I0168333

Instilling Aggressiveness
US Advisors and Greek Combat Leadership in the Greek Civil War
1947-1949

William D. Harris, Jr., Major, US Army

Combat Studies Institute Press
Command and General Staff College
Fort Leavenworth, Kansas

Abstract

In March 1947, the United States established an economic and military assistance program to bolster the nationalist Greek government against a communist insurgency. The Greek government suffered from a collapsed economy, deep social divisions, and an inability to defeat the insurgents in battle. The Joint US Military Advisory and Planning Group provided operational advice to the Greek National Army that improved the nationalists' aggressiveness, tactics, battlefield management, and logistics. The advisors used training, mentorship, directive control, and disciplinary action to affect the nationalists' combat leadership. The improved leadership led to more effective combat operations against the communists. These operations pressured the insurgency, which had alienated Yugoslavia and committed to fighting with conventional tactics. These two insurgent errors, the massive economic and military aid program, and the improved nationalist combat performance resulted in a decisive victory in August 1949. The study provides insight into how advisors can affect a military's leadership.

Acknowledgments

The author is indebted to the Art of War Scholars' seminar professors, Dr. Joseph Fischer, Dr. Sean Kalic, and Dr. Scott Stephenson, for hard work and dedication to professional military education. The author also thanks Dr. Joseph Babb and Dr. Nicholas Murray for their assistance with this thesis. The researchers at the President Harry S. Truman Library, the Military History Institute, and the National Archives and Records Administration provided valuable assistance to the author in conducting archival research. Most importantly, the author will be forever indebted to his loving wife for her patience and understanding.

Table of Contents

Illustrations

Acronyms

AMAG	American Mission for Aid to Greece
EAM	National Liberation Movement
EDES	National Republican Greek Association
GNA	Greek National Army
JUSMAPG	Joint US Military Advisory and Planning Group-Greece
KKE	Communist Party of Greece
NDC	National Defense Corps
RHAF	Royal Hellenic Air Force
SOE	Special Operations Executive
USAGG	United States Army Group-Greece

Chapter 1
Introduction

Is it not the manner in which the leaders carry out the task of command, of impressing their resolution in the hearts of others that makes them warriors?

— General Gerhard von Sharnhorst, *Infantry in Battle*

In 1947, at the dawn of the Cold War between the United States and the Soviet Union, the Greek Communist Party (KKE) had gained control of large portions of Greece and was threatening to defeat the nationalist royal Greek government. The nationalist Greek government faced numerous challenges. The Greek economy experienced the worst collapse of World War II under the weight of the Axis occupation. Greek society suffered from deep and violent cleavages that had originated before World War I. The government failed to rebuild the economy while many Greeks resisted the British backed return of the Greek King. Additionally, the KKE's military, the Greek Democratic Army, demonstrated that it was capable of defeating nationalist forces in open battle. In the midst of the escalating Cold War, President Harry S. Truman decided that the United States could not allow the communists to control Greece and the eastern Mediterranean Sea. In what the public called the Truman Doctrine, he announced a massive aid package to bolster the struggling Greek government to defend itself against the communist insurgency. The United States reinforced the Greek nationalists with weapons, supplies, financial support, and military advice. After two and a half more years of bitter fighting, the Greek nationalists achieved a decisive victory over their communist foes in September 1949.

The United States provided material aid, in the form of economic and military aid, was crucial for the nationalist victory. Additionally, two major KKE errors contributed significantly to the nationalist victory. However, the US military advisory mission's dramatic improvement of nationalist Greek combat leadership and effectiveness was essential to the decisive victory. The advisors improved the aggressiveness, tactics, battle control, and logistics through persistent training, mentorship, directive control, and influencing disciplinary action. Without the advisors' successful improvement of nationalist combat leadership, the Greek government would probably have squandered the US provided material aid and the communists could have recovered from their errors.

Literature Review

The majority of the academic literature on the Greek Civil War has focused on the communists' errors, although most of the research has included other factors as contributing causes. These other causes include US diplomatic efforts, US aid, and the Greek nationalists' efforts. The most balanced accounts briefly mention the US advisory effort, but emphasize material aid and argue that the communist errors were the deciding factor. They do not address which aspects of the GNA the advisors focused on to improve nationalist combat effectiveness or how the advisors improved those aspects.

One of the most detailed studies of the communist effort is Charles Shrader's meticulous study of the Democratic Army's organization. Shrader argues, "if one were forced to select a single explanation for the defeat of the GDA it would have to be inadequate logistics.[1]

The poverty of Greece and critical errors made by the communists leaders directly led to this logistical inadequacy. He lists four errors: not mobilizing the urban populations, harsh measures that alienated the population, the loss of Yugoslavian support, and the commitment of conventional tactics.[2] While Shrader briefly acknowledges that the United States was able to improve the nationalist forces, his argument is that the communist errors are more important to explaining the war's outcome. The KKE's ideological dedication to using conventional tactics was the most egregious of its errors because it sharply increased its logistical requirements while making it more likely to suffer high rates of attrition that the communist infrastructure could not overcome. The inadequate logistics resulted in an inability to generate and sustain enough combat power to defeat the nationalists in battle.[3]

Other authors besides Shrader have also focused on the communists' conventional tactics. Evangelos Averoff-Tossizza is a prominent example. He discounts the effect of losing Yugoslavian support, and focuses on the decision to build a conventional army instead of relying on guerrilla warfare.[4] The argument is that if the communists had focused on guerrilla tactics they could have overcome the other difficulties, including the US aid. Averoff-Tossizza does assert that it was the will of the Greek people that overcame the communists, which contradicts his argument that the communists could have changed the outcome of the war through better tactics. His political interests as an elected official may have influenced his discussion of the importance of the will of the people.[5]

Another study of the KKE, by Haris Vlavianos, details the KKE's inner workings and concludes that the party's errors prevented it from mobilizing the political support necessary for a revolution. Instead of focusing on the choice of conventional over guerrilla tactics, Vlavianos argues that the

KKE failed to wage revolutionary warfare as primarily a political effort, with the military supporting the mobilization of the people.[6] While this work presents an excellent window into the inner workings of the KKE, it does not address other potential causes as well as some other studies. Edgar O'Ballance concurs with Vlavianos, arguing that the communists' major fault was the "failure to win over the minds of the people."[7] His work does not have the same depth into the KKE that Vlavianos provides, but he does present a more balanced understanding of the war. O'Ballance's narrative discusses the nationalist military operations and he balances his argument by noting that the communists acquired momentum in 1946 and 1947 because the Greek government could not finance or equip a military large enough to overcome the communists. After 1947, the US aid program provided the necessary material for the nationalists to defeat the communists.[8]

The communists' errors arguments, especially those of Vlavianos and O'Ballance with their discussion of the KKE's political failures, are vulnerable to a critique presented by Stathis Kalyvas. Kalyvas argues that the civilians responded to control more than political narrative. The emphasis on the overarching narrative is a result of an "urban bias" that privileges the perspective of urban upper classes over the perspectives of the rest of the society, especially rural inhabitants. Consequently, arguments that claim that the communists failed to construct a suitable political narrative to win the people's allegiance ignore the complex web of local politics that had much more influence on how the people acted during the war than the lofty ideological statements. Kalyvas conducted extensive ethnographic research in the Argolid region of Greece as one test of his theory of control and violence. The research is limited to one region and mostly on the early phase of the Greek Civil War, 1944-1945. However, the fact that his research confirmed his theory that control mattered more than political preference in the Greek Civil War weakens the arguments of authors who argue that it was the will of the Greek people or communist political failings that determined the outcome of the war.[9]

The line of argument that focuses on the communist failures has made significant contributions to the scholarly understanding of the Greek Civil War. However, arguing that the communist errors were the proximate cause of the war's outcome requires problematic assumptions. It assumes that the issue is one of total victory for one side or the other. This assumption ignores the possibility that the KKE could establish an autonomous region in minority inhabited northern Greece. It also assumes away the possibility that the communists could perpetuate a stalemate that would make Greece a failed state. The communists' ability to generate at least twenty thousand fighters during 1949 demonstrates that the KKE had the organization, will, and discipline to continue fighting.[10] While the communist errors may have prevented them from achieving a total victory like Mao Tse-Tung's Chinese Communist Party, they could still have made it impossible for the Greek government to govern any locality outside of Athens. Averting the stalemate or autonomous region outcomes required the nationalists to take positive action to assert government control. As chapter 3 will demonstrate, the nationalists had no ability to do this in 1947 and most likely could not have done so without external assistance.

Christopher Woodhouse and Frank Abbott have argued that the US advisors did not have a significant effect on the outcome of the war. Instead, they argue that the Greek nationalists were able to reform themselves without the advisors' influence. The most prominent proponent of this view, Christopher Woodhouse, who led the British Military Mission in Greece during World War II, states that the US advisors did not provide any substantial assistance and that it was Greek officers who initiated the changes in nationalist tactics.[11] Woodhouse may have a conflict of interest since the US advisors took a much more aggressive role in GNA operations than the British advisors. Agreeing with Woodhouse, Frank Abbott flatly states that the US advisors failed to instill aggressiveness in the nationalist forces. He argues that the United States lost its leverage over the GNA when it made an unconditional commitment to the nationalist cause in the Truman Doctrine. Without this leverage, the US advisors could not motivate the Greek soldiers to fight aggressively. Only the arrival of a bold new commander, Field Marshall Alexander Papagos, in 1949 brought aggressiveness to the GNA.[12] The evidence in chapters 3 and 4 will show that the actual timeline of improvement in nationalist combat performance does not support the contention that the advisors played a marginal role.

Another study disputes the assertion that the United States lost leverage over the Greek government. Howard Jones, in the authoritative study of the strategic and diplomatic aspects of the Greek Civil War, argues that the Truman administration's strategic and diplomatic maneuvers were critical determinants of the war's outcome. Far from surrendering its leverage to the Greeks, the US executed a well-crafted strategy to respond to the apparent threat of communist expansion that deterred the Soviets and induced the nationalists to heed US advice. Jones does not discuss the KKE's operations and organization to the depth of Shrader or Vlavianos, but he does provide a balanced perspective of the war with a focus on US strategy and diplomacy. He does mention the US military advisors, but does not analyze their specific activities or effects in depth.[13]

4

In contrast to the works above, there is a group of studies that analyze the Greek Civil War but do not focus on explaining the outcome of the war. This group looks to the Greek Civil War as the beginning of a process that led to a 1967 military *coup*. Two prominent examples are Nicos Alivizatos and Yiannis Roubatis. Alivizatos contends that the Civil War caused a break down in the state institutions and increased military autonomy. These two effects would in turn lead to the collapse of democracy in 1967.[14] In a similar vein, Roubatis argues that the US involvement in Greek political and military affairs had long-term effects, including the *coup d'etat*.[15] Both of these authors are a part of a liberal revisionist movement in Greek historiography that arose after the 1974 restoration of democracy.[16] Their arguments provide important considerations for understanding the advisory mission in Greece and in future wars.

US Advisors and Greek Combat Leadership

This study focuses on the US military advisory effort's organization, actions, and effects on the GNA from 1947 to 1949. Although there were advisors for the Royal Hellenic Navy and the Royal Hellenic Air Force, the study will focus on the advisors to the army, which played the decisive role.[17] Chapter 2 details the origins of the Greek Civil War including the unique circumstances that contributed to the initial communist success. These circumstances include the long history of persistent guerrilla warfare in the Greek mountains, ethno-linguistic divisions, persistent poverty, and bitter political divisions. Greek expansion in two Balkan Wars led to the inclusion of non-Greek speakers who would provide willing recruits for the communists during the Civil War. World War I and its aftermath introduced the main political cleavage that would dominate Greek politics for the rest of the century and lead to the war. The Greek government went from crisis to crisis during the interwar years, reinforcing the central fissure. World War II brought an Axis occupation that ruined the economy and led to the beginning of the Civil War as the communist resistance movement sought to eliminate the other anti-occupation resistance groups. The British dealt a heavy blow to the communists and reinstalled the monarchy in 1945, but the communists recovered and fielded a new army that steadily expanded its control as the nationalist government suffered from economic collapse, misadministration, and poor military leadership.

Chapters 3 and 4 discuss the strategic situation, the communists' actions, the material situation, and the nationalist military with the US advisors. Chapter 3 covers the war from the announcement of the Truman Doctrine and the US mission to aid Greece in March 1947 until February 1948. The United States provided significant levels of material support in the form of economic and military aid to bolster Greece against the communist threat. Nevertheless, the communists continued to make progress, extending their control of rural Greece and successfully challenging GNA units in conventional battles. The deteriorating security situation led the Truman administration and the advisors in Greece to conclude that the GNA's combat leadership was the critical weakness in the nationalist cause. The advisors began a pertinacious emphasis on increasing nationalist combat leaders' aggressiveness, while the Truman administration prioritized military over economic aid and decided to provide operational advice to the GNA.

Chapter 4 covers the period from February 1948, when Lieutenant General James Van Fleet took command of the US advisory mission, to the September 1949 nationalist victory. The Truman administration worked to balance the domestic economy, the escalating Cold War, and the commitment to Greece. Internal machinations resulted in two critical KKE decisions that contributed to the communist defeat. The choice of conventional tactics committed the communists to a high-attrition form of warfare. Support for Macedonian independence alienated the KKE's Yugoslavian benefactors. Meanwhile, the US continued to sustain the GNA and provide new weapons. The advisors had an increasing effect on Greek combat leadership, instilling aggressiveness through training, mentorship, directive control, and discipline. The chapter analyzes how the advisors had this effect, the role of Marshall Papagos, and the inability of the communists to recover because of nationalist pressure. During the 1949 campaigns, the GNA demonstrated its newfound aggressive tactics through more effective operations that maintained a constant pursuit of the communist guerrillas. The war culminated in August 1949 with the final battles for the insurgent strongholds in Grammos and Vitsi.

Chapter 5 begins by discussing two long-term effects of the US influence on the Greek military, the mixed Greek performance during the Korean War and the military *coup d'etat* in 1967. The chapter presents observations about how the advisors affected Greek combat leadership. The next section reviews the causes of the decisive nationalist victory. The final section discusses the implications of these conclusions and suggests areas for future research.

Notes

1. Charles R. Shrader, *The Withered Vine: Logistics and the Communist Insurgency in Greece, 1945-1949* (Wesport: Praeger, 1999), 253.

2. Shrader, 256-257.

3. Shrader, While some insurgent ideologies, such as Maoism, are very flexible about tactics, the KKE followed a strict Stalinist line, which led the KKE's leaders to conclude that they had to win conventionally.

4. Evangelos Averoff-Tossizza, *By Fire and Axe* (New York: Caratzas Brothers, 1978), v-vii, 357-366.

5. Averoff-Tossizza.

6. Haris Vlavianos, *Greece, 1941-49: From Resistance to Civil War* (New York: St. Martin's Press, 1992), 8-11.

7. Edgar O'Ballance, *The Greek Civil War 1944-49* (New York: Frederick A. Praeger, 1966), 210.

8. O'Ballance, 210-220.

9. Stathis Kalyvas, *The Logic of Violence in Civil War* (Cambridge: Cambridge University Press, 2006), 38-48, 246-329.

10. Shrader, 119.

11. Christopher M. Woodhouse, *The Struggle For Greece, 1941-1949* (London: Hart-Davis, MacGibbon, 1976), 238.

12. Frank Abbott, "The Greek Civil War, 1947-1949: Lessons for the Operational Artist in Foreign Internal Defense" (Monograph, School of Advanced Military Studies, 1994), 37-41.

13. Howard Jones, *"A New Kind of War:" America's Global Strategy and The Truman Doctrine in Greece* (New York: Oxford University Press, 1989), 220-226.

14. Nicos C. Alivizatos, "The Greek Army in the Late Forties: Towards an Institutional Autonomy," *Journal of the Hellenic Diaspora* 5, no. 3 (Fall 1978): 37.

15. Yiannis Roubatis, *Tangled Webs: The US in Greece 1947-1967* (New York: Athens Printing Company, 1987), 7-9.

16. Stathis Kalyvas, "The Greek Civil War in Retrospect," *Correspondence* no. 4 (1999): 10-11.

17. For a study of air power see M. Campbell, E. Downs, and L. Schuetta, *The Employment of Airpower in the Greek Civil War, 1947-1949* (Maxwell Air Force Base: Air University, 1964).

Chapter 2
Background

The sufferings which revolution entailed upon the cities were many and terrible, such as have occurred and always will occur as long as the nature of mankind remains the same. . . . Revolution thus ran its course from city to city, and the places which it arrived at last, from having heard what had been done before, carried to a still greater excess the refinement of their inventions, as manifested in the cunning of their enterprises and the atrocity of their reprisals. . . . Thus every form of iniquity took root in the Hellenic countries by reason of the troubles.

— Thucydides, *The Peloponnesian War*

The roots of guerrilla war in modern Greece extend back to its modern independence, while the central political conflict that polarized the country began in the Balkan Wars and World War I. World War II led to increased communist influence, vast economic problems, further radicalization of Greek society, and a near communist victory that only British combat troops averted.[1] Post-war Greece found the communists rebuilding their insurgency while the government attempted to stabilize an economy in free-fall and field a new army and police force with British assistance

Modern Greece, 1821-1941

The Greeks have a long history of guerrilla, or bandit, warfare.[2] The Ottoman Empire never succeeded in extending its full control into the remote mountains of Greece. The people living in the ungoverned mountains had developed a culture of guerrilla warfare in which bands of armed men known as *klefts* made their living as brigands.[3] In the Greek War of Independence, these *klefts* provided much of the rebels' fighting strength. They also coerced the priests and major landowners in the towns to rebel. The entrance of Egypt on the side of the Ottomans and the constant factional fighting between different Greek leaders led to a crisis for the Greek cause in 1827. To increase their own influence in the eastern Mediterranean, the British, French, and Russians compelled the Ottomans to grant Greece its independence by destroying the Ottoman and Egyptian fleets at the battle of Navarino.[4] After three years of negotiations, all of the powers involved signed a treaty making Greece an independent state and a hereditary monarchy. The British, French, and Russians agreed that the new king would be the second son of the King of Bavaria. This arrangement kept Greece free of great power dynastic interests and hence it remained neutral.[5]

9

The Greeks fought several wars in the period between their independence and World War I, but it was the Balkan Wars immediately before the Great War that had the greatest impact on the future Civil War. In 1909 the army's Athens garrison threatened to mutiny unless the government acceded to demands for greater autonomy, a reduction of royal influence, and expansion of the military. This first of a long series of military interventions resulted in the rise of Eleftheios Venizelos, a liberal reformer, who the military accepted because he had proven his nationalist credentials in Crete and was not a part of the Athens political circles. Venizelos pushed through liberal economic reforms and pursued irredentist goals that brought Greece into the Balkan Wars of 1912-1913. Greece sought to seize territory in the Balkans and Asia Minor that had been Greek during classical times. Greece emerged from these wars with new lands in the north at Turkey's expense. Greece gained part of Macedonia, the region of Epirus in the northwest, and Thrace, a stretch of land to the northeast along the coast.[6] These new territories included non-Greek speakers who would provide a reliable base of support for the communists during the Civil War.

A dispute between Venizelos and King Constantine I in 1915 over which side to back in World War I shattered the sense of victory and unity in Greece. Venizelos believed in the Allied cause and their vague promises of a reward of the ethnically Greek portions of Asia Minor, while the king preferred to side with Germany. The pro-Venizelos and anti-Venizelos camps became bitterly divided. While the debate over World War I alliances was the surface issue the two camps divided over, the dispute involved many other issues as well. Supporters of the monarchy and economic policies that favored the status quo united against Venizelos. Liberals, reformers, opponents of the foreign royal family, and advocates of democracy supported Venizelos. This division drove the rise and fall of many governments, until the final victory of the royalist anti-Venizelos parties in 1936. This division would also provide a central cleavage for the Civil War.[7]

In addition to the conflict between the liberal Venizelos supporters and the conservative royalists, the outcome of World War I led to a war between Greece and Turkey and massive population movements in Greece. The collapse of the Greek Army that ended the war with Turkey led to the fall of Venizelos's government and the forced a massive population transfer between Greece and Turkey. This population movement and the integration of the northern territories Greece won during the Balkan Wars led to economic problems in a country that had languished economically for centuries.[8] Slavic-language speaking peoples, instead of Greek speakers inhabited these new territories. Additionally, the majority of the refugees from Asia Minor, who spoke Turkish, settled in the northern territories. These factors created a northern population in Greece that the Greek-speakers in the more affluent south suppressed and alienated, leading these northern areas to be a reliable base of support for the future communist movement.[9] The economic hardships led to the formation of the Greek Communist Party (KKE) in 1918.[10] The KKE had a poor showing at its first election in 1923, but continued to grow.[11]

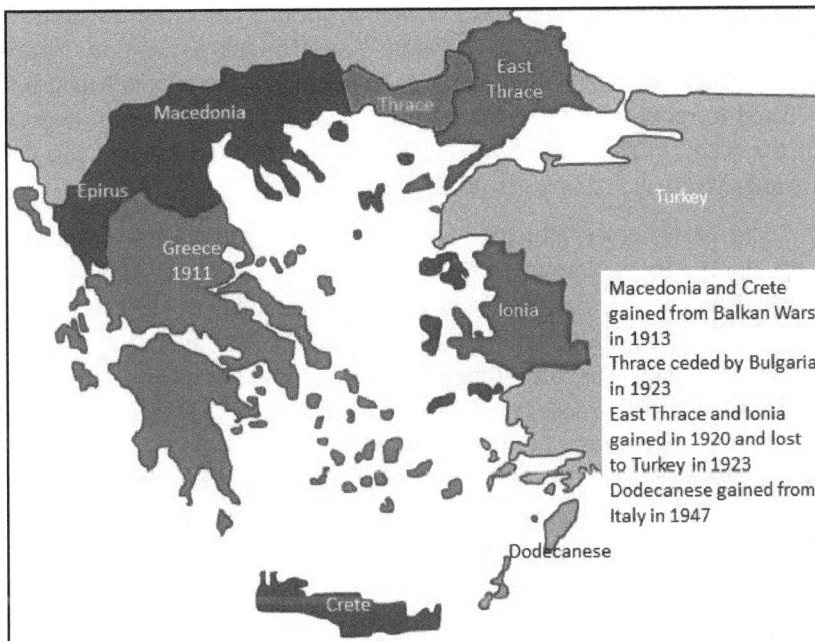

Figure 1. Map of Greek Territorial Expansion

Source: The author created the map based on information from Wikipedia, "History of Modern Greece," http://en.wikipedia.org/wiki/History_of_modern_Greece (accessed 8 August 2012).

The 1920s and early 1930s brought numerous governments and political chaos. In 1922, the king abdicated. His successor fled the country until a successful military *coup d'etat* reinstated him. There were also two other attempted *coups d'etats* in these chaotic years.[12] A 1924 national vote abolished the monarchy. Venizelos led the government for most of the decade, but failed to overcome the conservative resistance to his economic reform legislation. The absence of these reforms made Greece more vulnerable to the global depression and led to Venizelos' defeat in 1932.[13] This election ended the relative stability and political violence returned to Greece. Liberal Venizelos supporters in the military officer corps attempted two *coups d'etat*, the failure of which resulted in mass purges of liberal officers.[14] The liberals made the second attempt to prevent the restoration of the monarchy. In 1935, a group of senior officers led by General George Kondylis forced the Prime Minister, Panagiotis Tsaldaris, to restore the monarchy and resign.[15] The liberal and royalist parties closely contested the next general election in 1936. The economic conditions and new leadership had enabled the KKE to expand its official influence to over 100,000 votes in this election.[16] The close run race left the KKE as the party with the deciding votes. It made a coalition with the liberal party only for King George II to invalidate the results because he refused to reinstate purged liberal officers and was vehemently opposed to the KKE. [17] The king removed the elected government and installed Ioannis Metaxas, a dictator with fascist leanings.[18]

The Metaxas dictatorship, with a remit from the king to suppress opposition parties, strengthened the security services and cracked down on the KKE and Venizelists. Metaxas tried to emulate the fascist regimes in Germany and Italy, although his regime was not as effective as the National Socialists in controlling all of the country. His efforts to eradicate the KKE almost succeeded. The state jailed most of the leaders and obtained renunciations from most members, including tens of thousands who had never been members. The remaining KKE and Venizelist leaders dispersed into small cells to hide from the security services. Some of these cells survived the purge to provide the nucleus of the future anti-occupation resistance movements.[19]

In October 1940, Italy invaded Greece from the north after Metaxas refused Italian demands for basing concessions. The Greek army under command of General Alexander Papagos quickly defeated the Italians. The Italian offensive suffered from poor leadership, inferior artillery, the lack of coordination between land and ground operations, and undermanned units that were in the process of demobilization.[20] A few months later, the Greek government accepted British troops as a defense against a potential German attack. The attack came in April 1941 and pushed aside all resistance. The Germans, Italians, and Bulgarians occupied Greece by June. Most of the royalist officers fled with the king. In contrast, the surviving Venizelist and KKE cells remained and built a popular resistance movement to oppose the Axis occupation.[21]

The Occupation of Greece

The Axis powers established an occupation that divided Greece between German, Italian, and Bulgarian control. The Italians controlled most of the country while the Germans controlled Athens, Salonica, and other critical areas such as Crete. The Bulgarians occupied most of Thrace and began settling Bulgarian immigrants on Greek land. Initially the occupation deliberately attempted to conciliate the Greek populace. This effort included public statements about Greek courage and honor, release of all prisoners of war, and flying the Greek flag over all public buildings. Nevertheless, the Germans imposed a harsh occupation, appropriating most of the agricultural production and taxing the Greeks to pay for the occupation.[22] The resulting food shortage combined with a harsh winter caused 100,000 deaths during the winter of 1941-1942.[23] The Germans formed a Greek government under General Georgios Tsolakoglau, who had commanded a corps against the Italians in Albania.[24]

The King of Greece had fled with many of his government officials first to Crete and later to London. In addition to the British and Commonwealth forces, the British Royal Navy evacuated approximately 50,000 Greek officers and soldiers to Egypt, where they became the Free Greek Forces under British command.[25] General Papagos, averring that he could not flee his country when his men could not, naively believed German promises and surrendered. The Germans interned him in a concentration camp along with other political prisoners instead of releasing him with his sword as they did with other officers they had taken as prisoners of war.[26] While there were many soldiers who had not escaped from Greece, they did not immediately form a resistance movement. While there were scattered acts of resistance, including pulling down a swastika from the Acropolis in Athens, there was minimal resistance from the Greek people for the first few months.[27] The most significant act of resistance was the assistance the people provided to perhaps as many as 10,000 additional soldiers who eventually escaped from Greece. The people provided food, shelter and transportation to the soldiers who made their way to Greek civilian and British ships, which ferried them to safety in British territory.[28]

The Greek Communist Party prohibited its members from actively resisting the occupation, seeing the war as one between imperial powers. This view changed when the Germans attacked the Soviet Union on 22 June 1941. This attack led the KKE's Central Committee to commit to violent resistance to defend the Soviet Union. To achieve this purpose, they formed the National Liberation Front (EAM) in the autumn of 1941, with several other minor parties.[29] The EAM served as an umbrella organization to coordinate the efforts of all Greeks against the occupation. The KKE's leaders realized that their communist ideology was not resonating enough with the majority of Greeks, so they publically distanced themselves from the EAM. The KKE maintained secret control over the EAM's leaders.[30]

While the KKE was building the EAM, other Greeks began recruiting guerrilla bands in the tradition of the *klefts* and *andartes*. Colonel Napoleon Zervas was the guerrilla commander of the most effective of these other groups. A republican officer, he was the commander of the National Republican Greek Association (EDES). EDES and other guerrilla bands took to the mountains in central Greece beginning in the spring and summer of 1942.[31] The early actions of these groups spurred the EAM into forming its own guerrilla force. EAM had delayed the creation of its own guerrilla forces because of internal politics. The KKE members eventually accepted Aris Velouchiotis as the field commander even though he had renounced his association with the KKE during the Metaxas dictatorship.[32]

The *andartes'* early efforts had minimal effect on the occupation because the bands lacked training, supplies, and operational security. The British, through the Special Operations Executive (SOE) and the Secret Intelligence Service had begun operations in Greece in early 1941 to cooperate with the resistance.[33] The United States Office of Strategic Services would begin assisting the resistance in April 1944.[34] Most of these operations focused on smuggling Allied personnel out of occupied Europe. The SOE lost contact with its networks when Greece fell and did not reestablish contact until October, 1941. The early efforts of the British-sponsored networks had some successes including the sinking of several German tankers, but they also has several failures, including the capture of one British officer who under interrogation revealed the names of most of the politically moderate resistance leaders.[35] The British escalated their clandestine operations in Greece in October, 1942 as the military situation in North Africa became critical. They parachuted teams from the SOE into Greece to make contact with the *andartes* and assess the potential for interdicting the German traffic in Greece, which was providing the logistics for the Afrika Corps, which threatened British control of Egypt and the Suez Canal.[36]

The first team made contact with EAM elements, but the commander, Aris Velouchiotis, avoided contact with the British because he did not want to risk his forces in a dangerous assault.[37] Consequently, the British sent a second team to contact EDES. Zervas eagerly agreed to attack the

Gorgopotamos Viaduct, a choke point for all Axis supplies that crossed a deep gorge. When he learned that Zervas was moving his force to conduct the operation, Velouchiotis forced his way into the plan. The operation, which included a joint EDES and EAM attack on the garrison, while the British placed explosives, destroyed the bridge on 25 November 1942, although the delays meant that it came too late to affect the North African campaign.[38] The operation made EDES and EAM the two leading resistance movements and validated the SOE's concept for operations in Greece. The SOE, in contrast to the Secret Intelligence Service and the Greek government in exile, was willing to back the best resistance organization, regardless of politics. In Greece, this meant that the British government backed two anti-monarchal parties that fundamentally opposed to each other.[39]

Three factors increased the political separation between the royal government in exile and the resistance. First, the government's only liaison to the resistance died in a shootout after a betrayal in Athens on 12 August 1941. Second, after the death of the Greek liaison officer, the SOE controlled all communication between the government and the resistance. Several officers attempted to increase the Greek representation in planning meetings for supporting the resistance and inserting new liaisons. These officers eventually resigned from the King's service, leaving no advocate for a larger Greek role.[40] Third, the people increased their sympathy for the republicans and communists who suffered from the occupation alongside the people instead of living in exile.[41]

After the Gorgopotamos operation, the Greek resistance continued to grow. By January 1943, Zervas had recruited and trained 1,500 guerrillas, armed with British supplied weapons. EAM also increased its forces, although it frequently conscripted young men instead of persuading them. EAM spread its influence across the country, especially in the northern mountains of Macedonia and Salonika. It became the most popular resistance group, although the EDES still had more guerrillas and the British found that EAM would often delay operations indefinitely despite British rifles and gold. EAM, following the guidance of the KKE, was building its political foundation with the people before going on the offensive.[42] Some smaller *andartes* bands were more active. The Liberation Struggle Command, for example, under the command of Colonel Stephannos Saraphis, conducted effective operations with very small teams. EAM responded by capturing Saraphis under the pretext that Saraphis had been collaborating with the Italians. Once they had Saraphis in custody, they told him he that they would free him if he would become the EAM's military commander. [43] Saraphis agreed, seeing that EAM was now the strongest resistance organization in Greece. [44]

During the spring and summer of 1943, the *andartes* increased their recruitment and operations against the occupation. EAM began to order smaller guerrilla organizations to disband and join EAM. EAM's political infrastructure also increased recruitment in the towns, enabling it to grow to almost 14,000 guerrillas by August 1943, while EDES had only grown to 4,000. EDES did continue to maintain a qualitative advantage because former republican officers chose EDES over the communist influenced EAM. The Germans and Italians would reduce this EDES advantage through attrition because the occupation attacked EDES more than other *andartes* bands because of its higher level of activity and positions threatening the roads in Epirus. The British Military Mission, the organization that executed all British support for the resistance continually sought to coordinate and unify the competing resistance groups. The British Military Mission provided money and arms to the guerrillas in return for attacks against the Germans. The most important operation was Operation Animals, a coordinated offensive by all of the guerrillas that supported a British deception operation that sought to convince the Germans that the Allies would land in Greece instead of Sicily. This operation successfully induced the Germans to move three divisions into Greece. [45] Other British efforts were not so successful.

In August 1943, the British Military Mission transported delegates from each of the major groups to Cairo for a conference with the British command and the government-in-exile. The resistance delegates demanded that the king not return to Greece without a plebiscite calling for his return. King George II flatly refused and demanded that the conference end. The British government, which Prime Minister Winston Churchill had committed to the king's cause, supported the king's position, but continued its efforts to coordinate the angered guerrillas. The conference convinced the KKE and EAM that they needed to prepare for the post-war resistance by eliminating as much competition as possible, especially since the Italian surrender on 8 September 1943 and the battle of Stalingrad indicated that the Allies would win the war. [46]

The Civil War Begins

EAM started what scholars have named the first round of the Civil War by attacking EDES on 9 October 1943. [47] A strong EAM force attacked EDES strongholds in Epirus, forcing Zervas to pull his fighters from a series of defensive lines along rivers until he was able to counterattack.

But EAM's superior numbers enabled them to attack again in January 1943 bringing EDES to the point of destruction. At this point, the Germans intervened, fearing the communist EAM and preferring to keep the guerrillas fighting each other instead of allowing one group to dominate and coordinate the movement.[48]

Zervas kept his forces in the safe haven created by the German forces while the British government quickly worked to create a settlement to end the Civil War. The British Foreign Office, which was very suspicious of communist control of EAM, consistently pushed to end all aid to EAM, while the SOE emphasized the end to maintain pressure on the Germans. This bureaucratic difference was temporarily resolved in the name of creating a unified resistance. Meanwhile, the Foreign Office and Churchill tried to bring the exile government of George II to an agreement with the resistance. The resulting agreement, signed on 29 February 1944, ended the intra-Greek violence temporarily, but failed to resolve the critical constitutional issue, which was the status of the monarchy. The resistance groups, which were all anti-monarchal republicans or communists, wanted the king to remain outside of Greece until after a plebiscite on the king's status. George II refused.[49]

Seeing that the government in exile would never compromise, the KKE and EAM sought to solidify their political base. EAM's military leaders undertook a new campaign of violence against Greeks who failed to cooperate with EAM. EAM also created formed a new government, the Political Committee of National Liberation, in the northern mountains of Greece on 26 March 1944. This new government was solidly anti-monarchal and did not openly advocate communism. EAM's resistance activities earned the new government a degree of popularity with the people. This popularity extended to the Free Greek forces under British command. These units mutinied in April 1944, demanding recognition of the new government inside Greece. It took over a month for the British and the Greek exile government to suppress this mutiny, which broke the military forces and the exile government. The post-mutiny purge left the Free Greek Forces with one brigade and one commando battalion.[50]

With the invasions of continental Europe in France during June 1944, it became clear to the British officials responsible for Greece and the royal Greek government that they would have to enter Greece after a German withdrawal instead of an Allied liberation, meaning that EAM would control most of the territory unless the Allies rapidly occupied the country. This led the royalists to the conclusion that they would have to rely on the existing anti-communist forces in Greece. Since EAM had contained

EDES and suppressed most of the rest of the non-communist resistance organizations, the only strong anti-communist forces in Greece were the German created Security Battalions. Beginning in the fall of 1943, the German occupation authorities had begun a new counterinsurgency campaign based on anti-communism. The EAM offensives against EDES and used violence to compel cooperation from the people eventually led to a large number of recruits for these Security Battalions. The Security Battalions supported the Axis occupation by securing cities and roads against EAM attacks. Throughout 1944, volunteers continued to join the Security Battalions despite the fact that these units were surrogates of the occupation. Some of the recruits were former EDES members. Others were individuals that had collaborated with the occupation in other ways and saw the Security Battalions as a way to avoid punishment for their collaboration after the war. The British and the exile government reinforced this perception through their tacit approval of the Security Battalions. British radio broadcasts periodically prohibited resistance attacks against the Security Battalions. Word of clandestine meetings between the British and the Security Battalions quickly spread, reinforcing the perception that the Security Battalions would receive favorable treatment after the war.[51]

Concerns about the post-war fate of Greece, amplified by the mutiny of the Free-Greek Forces and the presence of the Soviet military in the Balkans, led Churchill to come to an agreement with Joseph Stalin over spheres of influence in May 1944.[52] Churchill ceded influence in Yugoslavia for a Soviet agreement to allow British dominance in Greece. Soviet officers arrived at the EAM headquarters in August 1944 and apparently influenced EAM into agreeing to the most recent power-sharing plan for post-war Greece.[53] These agreements however could not completely mitigate the inherent weakness of the royalist position in Greece. EAM had consolidated control over most of Greece. In September 1944, they attacked and destroyed most of the Security Battalion forces in the Peloponnese. This victory gave EAM control of all of Greece except EDES-held Epirus in northwestern Greece. The royalists and anti-communists were in a very weak position as the Germans prepared to withdraw. Most of the anti-communists were either tainted because they were anti-monarchal, had collaborated with the occupation, or both. The purge after the April 1944 mutiny had left the Greek National Army with only one brigade and one battalion, plus two fighter squadrons and a handful of naval ships. Additionally, the British could only spare two brigades to occupy Greece. This balance of forces presented the EAM with an opportunity to seize control of the whole country.[54]

The British Occupation and the Battle of Athens

The Germans withdrew their forces from Greece to reinforce other fronts in October 1944. As they slowly withdrew, the conventional Allied forces landed and occupied vacated territory. Fearing reprisals, most of the resistance chose to not fight the withdrawing Germans. The British and US advisors with the resistance, reinforced with some additional SOE and Office of Strategic Services forces, got a handful of units to attack the Germans to prevent the Germans from transferring all of their supplies out of Greece. EAM succeeded in capturing several stores of weapons and ammunition. Meanwhile, the exile government, under the Premier George Papandreau, returned to Athens with the British occupation forces and worked to tackle the myriad problems facing Greece.[55]

The government, with British help and relief supplies from the nascent United Nations, began to address the chronic food shortages, rampant diseases, massive unemployment, and dilapidated infrastructure. The most pressing problem, however, was the creation of new security forces. While EAM negotiated various agreements with the Papandreau government about integrating the various resistance organizations into a new army and police force, it was simultaneously creating its own security forces which controlled all of Greece except Epirus and the handful of cities with British garrisons. The crisis over demobilizing the resistance came on 1 December 1944 when EAM refused to integrate some of its units into the new military. The next day EAM staged a general strike and a massive protest in Athens, where the Free Greek Forces and the majority of the British were. The demonstration began peacefully, but as the protesters approached a police cordon, an unidentified police officer opened fire. The resulting skirmish left numerous civilians dead.[56] This bloodletting sparked escalating protests and EAM attacks on police positions. Three EAM divisions advanced into Athens. The EAM forces had quickly overpowered the Greek government, confining its power to only a small portion of Athens.[57]

By 5 December, the situation deteriorated to the point where the British, under orders from Churchill, intervened to prevent the resignation of the Papandreau government and issued an ultimatum to EAM to stop the attacks.[58] EAM refused to stop the fighting and pressed their advantage against the mostly incompetent government security forces. British troops, reinforced by two Indian brigades quickly transferred by air from Italy, assumed garrison duties from the Greek police. EAM units besieged the small British garrison, which only controlled three small sections of Athens, one of which was the critical airfield into which the reinforcements were arriving. On 10 December, the British and the Papandreau government decided to remove the existing sanctions on the former members of the Security Battalions and enlist them into the new security services. The British command also transferred an entire division from Italy to further reinforce its besieged units in Athens. With the weight of additional numbers and air support, the British slowly cleared Athens in house to house fighting against three EAM divisions. They did not clear the majority of Athens until New Years. The fighting continued until 15 January 1945 when a cease-fire took effect. Under the terms of the cease-fire, EAM withdrew from Athens, the Peloponnese, and Salonika. The British forces reoccupied these areas and turned them over to Greek forces.[59]

The Greek Democratic Army

EAM sued for a cease-fire because its leaders realized that the cost of fighting for Athens against the British had cost too many casualties. EAM demonstrated that it was a far more effective fighting force than the Greek nationalists, but many of their units had ceased to exist while fighting the British for Athens. Also, the loss led to conflicts within EAM's leadership ranks. Under the terms of the January truce and the subsequent political agreements, EAM disbanded and surrendered its weapons. The KKE core of EAM, however, was not prepared to disband.

The KKE leaders decided that they had to rebuild their military organization and reconsolidate their political position. The new military arm would be the Democratic Army of Greece. In building it, the KKE had several advantages. The KKE turned in less than half of EAM's weapons, concealing the remaining weapons in a series of caches throughout the mountains.[60] Five thousand KKE members and a number of other EAM veterans found refuge in Yugoslavia, Albania, and Bulgaria.[61] Additionally, the over one million displaced persons provided a potential recruitment pool.[62] The communists still controlled the mountains and many of the small towns, especially in the north.

The most important contributory factor in the growth of the Democratic Army was the wave of right-wing terror that swept the country after February 1945. There were a number of anti-communist terrorist groups, the most notorious being the "X" organization, that persecuted anyone associated with EAM. They murdered, tortured, and robbed former EAM members and their families. These organizations expanded their target lists to include moderate liberals who had opposed the Metaxas dictatorship or supported the republican Venizalist parties. The security services cooperated with the persecution.[63] Ultra-right wing officers gained influence in the new Nationalist Army. They prevailed in ensuring that former EAM members who had been brought into the Nationalist Army were put on the inactive list. Simultaneously, they brought more and more members of the Security Battalions into the security services. Remembering EAM's bloody methods during the resistance, many republicans who had opposed the monarchy came to see the King and the ultra-right wing officers who supported him as the only bulwark against a communist reign of terror. The white terror, as the right-wing campaign of violence was known, radicalized Greek society, driving individuals in the middle of the political spectrum to the extremes.[64]

The KKE had been focusing on political agitation, but the conclusion of the 15 December 1945 politburo meeting was that the KKE would need to respond militarily to the white terror. This meeting led to the formal creation of the Democratic Army on 12 February 1946. The old EAM quartermasters had been active since at least June 1945 preparing supplies for a new guerrilla force. Officers in the new Democratic Army began to build new units, visiting villages on recruiting trips and conducting training. [65] Following new instructions from Stalin, Yugoslavia, Albania, and Bulgaria offered increased support.[66] From July to December 1945, the Soviet Union indicated a changing position on the Balkans region through a series of diplomatic and military moves. These moves included calls to renegotiate the Montreux Convention, demands for Georgia and Armenia, request for naval bases in the Bosporus and Dardanelles, and a military move against Azerbaijan.[67] The KKE believed that it had Moscow's blessing to initiate hostilities.

The first attack by the new Democratic Army was on 30 March 1946, the eve of a general election, on a small town near Mount Olympus.[68] By late summer 1946, the Democratic Army regularly conducted guerrilla attacks on isolated outposts in the spirit of Greek guerrillas, *klefts*, and *andartes* throughout Greek history. The military commander, Vaphiados Markos, ordered an escalation in October 1946. This escalation focused on larger guerrilla unit attacks, up to 400 fighters, that would seize villages, kill the security forces personnel and other marked individuals, collect food and supplies, and withdraw when the reinforcements arrived. These reinforcements were often so slow that the guerrillas held the villages for days before a relief column came near.[69]

Markos put an emphasis on increasing the size of the Democratic Army so that it could contest all of Greece. By December 1946, it controlled large portions of northern Greece as well as many of the mountain ranges throughout the rest of the country. By recruiting former EAM guerrillas, Markos expanded the Democratic Army to approximately five thousand by October 1946. Further recruiting and conscription doubled that number again by the end of 1946. By establishing training camps and continuing recruitment during the winter, Markos had an army of 13,000 with varying levels of training by March 1947. To supply this expanding military, Markos visited the capitals of his allies Yugoslavia, Albania, and Bulgaria. While the aid from these countries was much less than requested, it did enable Markos to continue offensive operations. The allied countries provided space for camps and supplies that enabled the Democratic Army to build a series of secure bases in the mountains near the border.[70] Two years after the disastrous Battle of Athens, the communists had rebuilt a military and had seized the initiative from the Greek Government, which was struggling with a host of economic and material problems.

The Material Situation

Greece emerged from World War II in desperate straits that only got worse in the first post-war years. The Greek economy was already weak before the axis invasion because it had not industrialized and had been in default for half of the years since independence.[71] The Germans appropriated as many foodstuffs and other supplies as they could during their occupation, contributing to the starvation. The occupation also destroyed a quarter of all buildings in the country while the civil war and the Battle of Athens interrupted the minimal trade that had survived. The war led to the deaths or chronic disability of 19 percent of the population.[72] In the words of a US report on the Greek economy, "Greece today faces a desperate economic crisis – one that she cannot meet alone."[73]

The Greek government, in part because it had gone through seven actual governments during 1945 and 1946, was failing to sustain the economy or raise revenue to pay for the government. The government's budget was three times the total amount of currency available in the economy, let alone revenue the government could actually generate. Despite 700 million dollars of international aid in 1945 and 1946, the economy was failing.[74] A cycle of hyperinflation ensnared the economy. In 1944, the Greek currency, the drachma, had entered into the worst currency crash in world history and the crash was still disabling the country's ability to function.[75] By January 1947, agricultural production began to recover and approached its pre-war levels, but industrial production stagnated and the country's infrastructure faced a "reconstruction problem of immense proportions."[76] The economic collapse meant that the government could barely function and faced severe difficulties in fielding competent security forces.

The Greek Nationalist Army

The Greek government returned to Greece with one brigade and one battalion. The brigade was a mountain infantry brigade that had earned the name "Rimini Brigade" during the capture of Rimini, Italy.[77] During this battle, its first, the Greek brigade fought courageously despite its inexperience. However, the Greeks were slow on the offensive and relied on frontal attacks. The independent battalion was the "Sacred Band," an elite formation that fought alongside the British Special Air Service in North Africa.[78] The British Military Mission took the lead in creating a new nationalist army for Greece and used these two units as the officer cadre for three new divisions.[79] These officers were extremely loyal to the crown, having survived the purges of politically suspect moderates after the April 1944 mutiny. These politically aware officers collaborated with clandestine right-wing organizations that sought to use violence and harsh punishments against anyone tainted with communism or republican ideas.[80]

The three senior British advisors, who had non-voting seats in the Supreme Council of National Defense, helped design a force structure that quickly expanded to almost 100,000 soldiers by the end of 1946. This rapid expansion, however, meant that many of the conscripted soldiers deserted and the officers trusted few of the remaining soldiers since the officers suspected them of having communist or liberal sympathies. The Democratic Army's escalating operations led to an increase in the police and then arming of village home guards. In the minds of many civilians, widespread extortion and murder (frequently for revenge against EAM) tainted the security forces. The nationalist army committed most of its forces to static defense, even prohibiting units from leaving their post to relieve other units that were under attack. When the army did undertake offensive operations, they took the form of massive clearing operations conducted in accordance with a strict timetable. The forces would leave a village after a set period, no matter the results of the operation at that point. To hold the village, the army only left a handful of gendarmes, a force too weak to resist any guerrilla attack. This meant that the guerrillas retained the initiative, able to avoid contact whenever they chose to.[81]

The nationalist army suffered other problems as well. The nationalist army so centralized its command authority that division commanders could not move any units without approval.[82] The bankrupt government could barely sustain, pay, train, and equip its rapidly expanded army, let alone an air force and a navy. The army did not have enough trucks to move its forces or food to feed them. The army was also required to support 7,000 soldiers who the army confined to an island prison camp because the royalist government suspected their loyalties.[83]

All of these problems compounded as casualties rose from the guerrilla attacks that destroyed the isolated units on static defense and killed civilians that provided intelligence to the government. While the Greek army defeated the Italians in 1940, it steadily declined to the point of crisis in 1947. The purge of moderate and liberal officers and noncommissioned officers reduced the number of qualified leaders. The politicization increased until "the officer corps was honeycombed with secret leagues and associations."[84] Repeated purges and the interference of politicians in officer personnel decisions undermined the GNA's tactical effectiveness.[85] Additionally, while many of the communist officers gained valuable experience World War II, the Free Greek Forces that formed the basis of the GNA fought only one short campaign in Italy. The GNA's rapid expansion between 1945 and 1947 also reduced the GNA's effectiveness by diluting the already scarce combat experience. The decline in nationalist combat effectiveness by the winter of 1946-1947 led to a crisis for the Greek government. The KKE and its Democratic Army had a growing momentum.

Summary

The Greek nation, with its long history of guerrilla war had a government that was struggling to stabilize the economy and security situations. The division between the liberals and royalists that began just before World War I radicalized society with decades of bloodshed. The deleterious effects of World War II compounded an already weak economy and left the state with few resources on which to draw to combat the communist threat. All of these factors resulted in a military that was paralyzed and unable to defeat the Democratic Army.

Notes

1.   Andre Gerolymatos, *Red Acropolis, Black Terror* (New York: Basic Books, 2004), 143-147.

2.   The nationalist government labeled the communist guerrillas bandits and used the term bandit warfare.

3.   Richard Clogg, *A Concise History of* Greece (Cambridge: Cambridge University Press, 1992), 15.

4.   The War of Independence was also the first US involvement in a Greek war. In the spirit of philhellenism, the US government provided moral support, private citizens donated money, and a few traveled to Greece to fight in the rebel forces. One American rose to the rank of Lieutenant General in the Greek Army. Concerns about lost trade with the Ottoman Empire and a possible European response in the western hemisphere convinced President James Monroe to reverse his announced decision to send military aid. Michael B. Oren, *Power, Faith, and Fantasy* (New York: W. W. Norton and Company, 2007), 107-111.

5.   Clogg, 42-48.

6.   Barbara Jelavich, *History of the Balkans Vol 2 Twentieth Century* (Cambridge: Cambridge University Press, 1999), 95-100.

7.   Clogg, 86-93.

8.   Jelavich, 406; Clogg, 105-108.

9.   Stathis N. Kalyvas, *The Logic of Violence in Civil War* (Cambridge: Cambridge University Press, 2006), 311.

10. Averoff-Tossizza, 7-8.

11. Vlavianos, 8-11.

12. Clogg, 103-119.

13. Vlavianos, 11.

14. Clogg, 116.

15. Gerolymatos, *Red Acropolis*, 13.

16. Vlavianos, 10.

17. Gerolymatos, *Red Acropolis,* 27-30.

18. Gerolymatos.

19. Averoff-Tossizza, 31-36; Gerolymatos, 29-30.

20. Williamson Murray and Alan Millett, *A War to be Won: Fighting the Second World War* (Cambridge, MA: Harvard University Press, 2000), 95-98.

21. Clogg, 121-123; Gerolymatos, *Red Acropolis*, 32-39.

22. Gerolymatos, *Red Acropolis*, 46-47.

23. Clogg, 123-125.

24. O'Ballance, 47.

25. Gerolymatos, *Red Acropolis*, 45; Averoff-Tossizza, 57.

26. Averoff-Tossizza, 57-58.

27. Clogg, 125.

28. Averhoff-Tossizza, 57.

29. The exact date is unknown. The KKE claimed that it was formed on 27 September 1941, but KKE documents do not mention the EAM until later in 1941. Kousoulas, 149. For simplicity, this paper will use EAM for both the Front and its military arm, the National Popular Liberation Army (ELAS is most of the literature). The military arm was officially created on 22 May 1942. Gerolymatos, 73.

30. O'Ballance, 50.

31. Clogg, 129; O'Ballance, 53.

32. Kousoulas, 149.

33. Gerolymatos, *Red Acropolis*, 60-63.

34. Richard H. Smith, *OSS: The Secret History of America's First Central Intelligence Agency* (Guilford, CT: The Lyons Press, 2005), 116-117.

35. This unfortunate event contributed to the decline of the moderates in Greek political life, contributing to the beginning of the Civil War. Gerolymatos, *Red Acropolis*, 60-65.

36. O'Ballance, 55.

37. Kousoulas, 156.

38. Hugh Gardner, *Guerrilla and Counterguerrilla Warfare in Greece, 1941-1945* (Monograph, Washington, DC: Office of the Chief of Military History), 79-86.

39. Gerolymatos, *Red Acropolis*, 72-78.

40. Clogg states that the government-in-exile chose not to support the resistance because sabotage would only increase the suffering of the people; Clogg, 129.

41. Gerolymatos, *Red* Acropolis, 68-70.

42. Kousoulas, 158-160.

43. O'Ballance, 58-59.

44. Averoff-Tossizza, 84-85. This seemingly easy and quick change of heart is a bold claim. Averoff-Tossizza claims to have access to Saraphis's relatives who support his claim about Saraphis's motivations.

45. Gerolymatos, *Red Acropolis*, 81-83.

46. Kousoulas, 169-172.

47. Clogg, 132.

48. Gerolymatos, *Red Acropolis*, 85-86.

49. Averhoff-Tossizza, 93-96; Gerolymatos, *Red Acropolis*, 85-88.

50. Gerolymatos, *Red Acropolis,* 89.

51. Andre Gerolymatos, "The Security Battalions and the Civil War," *Journal of the Hellenic Diaspora* 12, no. 1 (Spring 1985): 17-27.

52. They negotiated the settlement in May 1944, but did not make it official until October 1944. Clogg, 133.

53. Clogg, 134-135.

54. Averohoff-Tossizza, 106-110; O'Ballance, 87.

55. O'Ballance, 88-89.

56. Gerolymatos, *Red Acropolis*, 99-107.

57. O'Ballance, 97.

58. Gerolymatos, *Red Acropolis*, 113.

59. O'Ballance, 98-108; Clogg, 137; Averhoff-Tossizza, 115-127; fatally, EAM diverted a significant amount of its fighters from Athens to Epirus to destroy EDES. While it destroyed EDES, EAM did not have enough combat power to seize the last few blocks of Athens before the British reinforcements arrived. Averhoff-Tossizza, 129-131.

60. Averhoff-Tossizza.

61. Gerolymatos, *Red Acropolis*, 205.

62. Gerolymatos, 196.

63. Vlavianos, 79-80.

64. Andre Gerolymatos, "The Road to Authoritarianism," *Journal of the Hellenic Diaspora* 35, no. 1 (Spring 2009): 14-17; O'Ballance, 115.

65. O'Ballance, 121-123.

66. Gerolymatos, *Red Acropolis*, 208-209.

67. Kousoulas, 230.

68. Gerolymatos, *Red Acropolis*, 209-210.

69. O'Ballance, 128-130.

70. O'Ballance, 131-133.

71. Carmen M. Reinhart and Kenneth S. Rogoth, *This Time is Different: Eight Centuries of Financial Folly* (Princeton: Princeton University Press, 2008), 98.

72. Gerolymatos, *Red Acropolis*, 196.

73. Paul A. Porter, "American Economic Mission to Greece," Papers of Paul A. Porter, Harry S. Truman Presidential Library, Independence, MO, 5-6.

74. Porter, 2.

75. Reinhart and Rogoth, 12.

76. Porter, 18-21.

77. The battle began on 13 September 1944 with German attacks from their Gothic defensive line. Attached to the 2 New Zealand Division, the Greeks withstood several attacks by German paratroopers from the 1 Parachute Division and Turkoman (foreigners, mostly Czarist Russians or Turkic soldiers from the Soviet Union) troops from the 162nd Division. The New Zealand 22 Motor Battalion reinforced the Greeks providing tank support. The Greeks advanced slowly with support from Canadian and New Zealand forces. British Commonwealth units seized San Marino and the ridge overlooking Rimini on 20 September, which led the Germans to conclude that their Rimini positions were untenable. On 21 September, Greek and New Zealand forces entered Rimini after the Germans withdrew from the city. The New Zealanders' official history noted the Greeks courage, especially in the defense. It also records slow Greek offensives, inexperienced troops, high casualty rates, frontal assaults, and difficulty with combined arms. These traits would also characterize the future Greek nationalist forces. Jim Henderson, *22 Battalion*, The Official History of New Zealand in the Second World War 1939-1945 (Wellington, New Zealand: Historical Publications Branch, 1958), http://nzetc.victoria.ac.nz/tm/scholarly/tei-WH2-22Ba.html (accessed 15 November 2012), 341-347; Robin Kay, *Italy Volume II: From Casino to Trieste*, The Official History of New Zealand in the Second World War 1939-1945 (Wellington, New Zealand: Historical Publications Branch, 1958), http://nzetc.victoria.ac.nz/tm/scholarly/tei-WH2-2Ita.html (accessed 15 November 2012), 211-227.

78. The unit was named after the famed Theban Sacred Band, which may date back to the battle of Plataea in 479 BC, where, "keen to fight . . . 300 of the best and most prominent of [the Thebans] fell." Herodotus, *The Landmark Herodotus*, Translated by Robert B. Strassler (New York: Pantheon Books, 2007), 698.

79. Kousoulas, 229.

80. Alivizatos, 40.

81. Kousoulas, 241; O'Ballance, 129; Gerolymatos, *Red Acropolis*, 222.

82. O'Ballance, 129.

83. United States Army Group Greece, "Official History of the United States Army Group Greece," Harry S. Truman Presidential Library, Independence, MO, Records Group 407: records of the Adjutant General's Office, 1917, Boxes 39-40, 47, 98-99.

84. Thanos Veremis and Andre Gerolymatos, "The Military as a Sociopolitical Force in Greece, 1940-1949," *Journal of the Hellenic Diaspora* 17, no. 1 (1991): 115.

85. Veremis and Gerolymatos, 117-120.

Chapter 3
The Truman Doctrine and the Beginning of the US Mission
March 1947-February 1948

> But to capitalize on this effort GNA must come alive and GNA commanders must take aggressive action.
>
> — Brigadier General Reuben Jenkins, Cable to VIII Division

In response to the threat of communist expansion around the globe, the United States government quickly created the American Mission for Aid to Greece (AMAG) in Greece to organize its assistance efforts to the besieged Greek nationalist government. The administration initially focused this mission on rebuilding the economy and material support for the nationalist army. The massive infusion of material and political support from the United States to Greece did not improve the Greek security situation by the end of 1947. Despite 300 million dollars of the US aid in the form of everything from weapons and rations to planes, the nationalist army was still not able to defeat the communist Democratic Army in the field or separate them from the rural population. A growing sense of failure led by the end of 1947 to a decision that the United States would have to expand and alter its assistance program to provide operational advice to the nationalist military to defeat the communist guerrillas.

Strategic Situation

After World War II, the relationship between the Soviet Union and the United States deteriorated into the Cold War, a period of hostility short of open warfare. After the British government announced that it could no longer afford to assist the Greek government combat the KKE, the Truman administration decided to implement the Truman doctrine to prevent the spread of communism.

Beginning of the Cold War

Relations between the Soviet Union and the United States after World War II became more hostile. US officials working with the Soviet Union had begun feeling frustrated with their supposed allies even during the war.[1] Attempts by the Truman administration to first win Soviet trust and then to bargain over influence in different parts of the world failed to achieve stable agreements. The first approach assumed that the problem in Soviet relations was that the Soviet Union did not trust the United States, so more transparency would alleviate the problem. The second approach assumed that the Soviet Union would make deals with the United States in exchange for aid. These attempts failed because the United States did not have sufficient leverage to get the Soviets to agree to the United States' positions.[2] George Kennan, a Foreign Service officer who would later help formulate the administration's policies toward Greece, attributed the Soviet intransigence to their domestic political structure in a 1946 telegram that quickly gained the approval of the administration.[3] This telegram and a subsequent article in *Foreign Affairs* suggested a long-term strategy to contain Soviet aggression while ensuring the "health and vigor" of western civilization until the internal nature of the Soviet state changed.[4]

The Soviets began challenging US interests in the greater Mediterranean region in 1946. In August, they renewed their interest in more influence in Turkey, including demanding joint control over the Bosporus and Dardanelles Straits. Yugoslavia also demanded territory from Italy, while Bulgaria demanded the return of Thrace from Greece. While the Truman administration rebuffed these communist demands, the incessant communist expansion troubled the administration. The dispute over Turkey led to a September 1946 State Department report that recommended a firm policy against Soviet expansion.[5]

Throughout the rest of 1946, several Soviet actions indicated to the United States that the Soviet Union had aggressive intentions in Greece and around the world. US intelligence acquired access to meetings in which communist officials indicated that they were embarking on a path of communist expansion by all means short of general war. An intelligence report in December 1946 led the Truman administration to conclude that Greece would be the first target.[6] Communist propaganda increasingly focused on the shortcoming of Greek democracy and the rampant abuses of power by the royalist Greek government.[7] While the administration did not have proof of Soviet complicity in the Greek communist insurgency, it did have evidence of Yugoslavian, Albanian, and Bulgarian support. Moreover, it suspected that Moscow would keep its hands clean until the communists had achieved control over at least a sizeable portion of Greece.[8]

The Soviet Union at a minimum provided diplomatic support to the KKE. When the Greek government asked the United Nations Security Council to investigate aid for the guerrillas flowing across the northern Greek borders, the Soviet Union initially blocked any investigation. When they did acquiesce to the creation of a Balkan Commission, the Soviet representative on the commission attempted to disrupt the commission's investigation. Yugoslavia, Albania, and Bulgaria refused to allow the commission to cross into their territory to conduct the investigation.[9] The

Soviet members on the commission worked to keep the commission in Athens and expand its scope to look at the abuses of the Greek government.[10]

By the beginning of 1947, there was a general consensus in the Truman administration that the Soviet Union and its communist allies in the Balkans were using subversion to expand southward into Greece and Turkey.[11] Furthermore, the administration had concluded that successful communist control of these two countries would threaten US access to the Middle East, which in turn would threaten the United States economy.[12] The continued failures of the Greek government, including its inability to accommodate political moderates, defeat the growing number of communist guerrillas, or stabilize its economy made the United States' interests in the region vulnerable.[13]

The Creation of the Truman Doctrine

The British government, while it had been the principal power buttressing the nationalist Greeks against the communist threat, concluded that it would have to pull out of Greece because of its urgent fiscal difficulties. On 21 February 1947, the British Government told the Truman administration that it could no longer afford its aid program to Greece.[14] This letter led the Truman administration to a series of policy studies that quickly led to the conclusion that the US could not allow the communists to control Greece.[15] This message sped up a process of increasing US aid for Greece that had been slowly building momentum. Because of the increasing communist threat to Greece, the Secretary of State, George Marshall, sent Paul A. Porter to Greece in January 1947 to assess the level of US aid necessary to stabilize the Greek economy. Porter's report provided the basis for organizing and appropriating funds for the AMAG. Porter concluded that the United States would need to contribute at least 350 million dollars (equivalent to three and a half billion dollars in 2012 terms).[16]

However, the obvious failings of the Greek government caused the Truman administration to delay its new aid program until the British withdrawal announcement created a new sense of urgency. Porter and Marshall were concerned that the Greek government was too oppressive and too reactionary to be a good partner for the United States. US Ambassador Lincoln MacVeagh was more supportive of the Greek government, but believed that it had to incorporate the opposition parties.[17] The royalist Populist Party dominated the Greek government, which alienated a large percentage of the people including all of the moderates through harsh treatment in the name of anti-communism. In the words of a report by the office of Governor Dwight Griswold, who would lead the US mission in Greece, the Greek government had "adopted a policy of repression."[18] Individuals who cooperated with the Metaxas dictatorship and the Axis occupation dominated the Populist Party.[19] Napoleon Zervas, who had commanded EDES and became an example of the ultra-right-wing officials, was implementing such repressive measures by right-wing terrorist groups that he was "making more communists than he [was] eliminating."[20] King George II's attitude of "condescension" toward the Greek people, with no "genuine passion for improving the welfare or living standards of the people," may have reinforced this pervasive government attitude of harsh measures.[21]

The potential to lose Greece after the British withdrawal and some Greek efforts to ameliorate the Truman administration's concerns about their domestic politics influenced a rapid decision-making process in the Truman administration. Within days of the British announcement, the administration had decided to implement a major aid package for Greece and Turkey. After gaining the support of crucial leaders in the Congress, President Truman announced what came to be called the Truman Doctrine and requested a comprehensive program in an address on 12 March 1947 to a joint session of the Congress. The Congress passed Public Law 75, which authorized economic and military aid, to include "a limited number of members of the military . . . in an advisory capacity only."[22]

Under the authority of this new law, the State Department established a new organization, the American Mission for Aid to Greece (AMAG). The President appointed Governor Dwight Griswold as the Chief of Mission. This led to an awkward arrangement since the United States would have two Chiefs of Mission in Greece, Griswold and Ambassador Lincoln MacVeagh. Both were personal representatives of the President. In an attempt to delineate responsibilities, the administration eventually told Griswold to limit his activities to administering the aid program and leave political advice to MacVeagh. The administration told both men that the US interest in Greece was preventing the Soviet Union from controlling Greece, which would deny the US access to the strategically important Aegean and eastern Mediterranean Seas and grant it to the Soviet Union access.[23] The instructions to the Chief of the American Mission for Aid to Greece specified the US objectives in Greece as the "maintenance of the independence and integrity of Greece, specifically to keep Greece from falling into the Soviet orbit; and development of the economy of Greece on a self-sustaining basis as soon as possible."[24] The State Department was also concerned that a communist victory in Greece would influence the 1948 elections in Italy in favor of the communists, which in turn would bolster the communist party in France.[25]

Despite the gravity of the threats to US national interest in Greece, there were significant limitations on America's commitment. Within months of President Truman's announcement of programs aid to Greece and Turkey, political pressure began building to reduce these programs in the name of easing economic conditions inside the United States. Senator Robert Taft (Republican, Ohio) led the opposition, saying that the President preferred to spend money abroad rather than bring down prices at home.[26] The administration had apparently anticipated these problems in creating the aid programs. Despite the lofty language in Truman's speeches, the planning assumptions for the aid program included two very optimistic assumptions. The first assumption was that the Greek army would be able to "suppress armed resistance and restore internal order" by the end of 1947. The second assumption was that AMAG would have "reasonable success reform[ing] public administration."[27] The Truman administration faced competing priorities. To expand the Greek security forces and execute major reconstruction project required more funding, but the Greek government could not afford its current expenditures. Without major cuts in Greek defense spending, the Truman administration would have to commit between 125 and 135 million dollars in 1947 alone just to keep the Greek government solvent, let alone balancing the Greek budget.[28] Influential voices inside the administration, including Kennan, repeatedly sought to limit US military involvement because of the dangers of being trapped in an undesirable military conflict if it made too great of a military commitment to Greece.[29] The administration would have to balance this against the need to support the domestic economy and limit liabilities around the world. This tension led the administration to hope for a quick victory and reduced budgets for its Greek program.

The Greek Communists

This section will explain how the KKE and its Greek Democratic Army gained momentum throughout 1947. The government security forces were unable to prevent the communists expanding their control of rural Greece or executing attacks in the cities. Although they did not achieve all of their goals and had some tactical defeats, the communists increased their armed force by 500 percent, which contributed to a sense of momentum by the winter of 1947-1948.

Creation of Communist Controlled Zones

With the creation of the Greek Democratic Army in October 1946, the communists embarked on a strategy of controlling territory that they could deny to nationalist forces. The most important stronghold for the communists was in the Grammos and Vitsi Mountains. These mountains controlled access to the borders with Yugoslavia and Albania. They were also some of the most imposing mountains in Greece. Markos, the military commander of the Democratic Army, established his command post and ordered his logistics units to start stockpiling concealed supply stores in the Grammos area. The guerillas used this strategically important area as a base until the end of the war. To deny access to the nationalist forces, the communists used mines, bunkers, anti-tank weapons, and anti-aircraft artillery.[30]

The communists expanded this control in the rural mountains across Greece, especially in the north. Rough, constricted, mountainous terrain covers 60 percent of Greece, making it relatively easy for mobile guerrillas to block roads and isolate small nationalist units.[31] Frequently they used small operations to attack isolated government positions, government officials, informants, and right-wing terrorists. The communists expanded these zones in a general eastward line from the Albania border, which provided them secure lines of communication into much of Greece and threatened to isolate northern Greece from government forces. Small raids attacked villages to kill government officials, acquire food and supplies, seize weapons and ammunition, and coerce the population to not cooperate with the government.[32] When attacking a military position, they generally conducted a "quiet infiltration of the perimeter of Nationalist positions, followed by an assault on both the outer defenses and the main body of defending troops . . . [then a] withdraw under cover of machine and mortar fire."[33]

Once they forced the government to withdraw its forces from a village, the communists established a uniformed home guard. These units maintained order in the villages, provided logistical support for the regular insurgent units, and punished those who cooperated with the government. In secure areas, the communists established bases. They relied on concealment to protect these bases instead of overt defense. In areas that the guerrillas had not secured, they organized clandestine groups of villagers to collect information and supplies for local guerrillas.[34]

In the spring 1947, the communists began a new willingness to engage in battle with the government forces in an attempt to expand their zone of uncontested control in the northern mountains. The guerrillas conducted successful spoiling attacks against a major GNA operation in June 1947. The purpose of this fifteen-battalion GNA operation was to occupy a line of villages that paralleled the Albanian border. The GNA claimed to have inflicted 300 casualties on the insurgents, a heavy toll for the insurgents. Nevertheless, the attack did force the Greek General Staff to commit another corps, B Corps, to continue the operation.[35]

In response to the continued operation, on 12 July 1947, a column of approximately 2,500 Democratic Army soldiers crossed the border from Albania into Greece, isolated and captured the border town of Konitsa. The communists continued their advance for three days and thirty miles until the Government forces finally checked the communist progress at the town of Kalpaki. This column was well supplied with mule trains and heavy weapons.[36] The GNA eventually defeated these major communist attacks, but not without difficulty. Moreover, the scale of the attacks called into question the ability of the GNA to defeat the communists. On the other hand, the repeated assaults on government positions led to significant casualties for the communist forces. These repeated assaults and their high casualties were the result of a deliberate decision to challenge the nationalists with a conventional military. The KKE leaders' Stalinist ideology led them to believe that the Democratic Army had to win in conventional battle.

Building the Democratic Army

These major operations were the result of the KKE's policy of expanding and transforming the Democratic Army into a conventional military capable of seizing and defending territory. This transformation slowly integrated the dispersed guerrilla bands into companies of sixty to eighty men, into battalions by January 1948 and finally into brigades and divisions. The KKE decided on this conventional military policy during several meetings during 1946 and 1947 over the objections of the military commander Vafiadis Markos. The KKE's political leader, Nikos Zachariadas, was a devoted Stalinist and wanted to model his Democratic Army on the Red Army.[37]

In communist controlled areas, the Democratic Army established training camps and logistical units. According to one estimate, the Democratic Army averaged 8,000 officers and soldiers in military schools at any given time. Many of these facilities were in the communist states to the north, especially the officer and technical schools, but there were local training camps for each regional command. The insurgents also recruited or drafted villagers to fill their expanding ranks and to replace casualties. As the nationalist forces attrited their pool of willing volunteers, the insurgents increasingly used conscription to fill their ranks. Throughout 1947 and into 1948, the communists were able to find enough recruits to field a force of over 20,000 regulars, in addition to at least 70,000 auxiliaries.[38]

As of 1 January 1948, the KKE had organized the Democratic Army around battalions consisting of 200-300 infantrymen. Three battalions composed a regiment, which also had a heavy machine gun company. In some of the twenty-five area commands, the commanders had begun forming divisions of three regiments each. The twenty-five area commands were divided into four regional commands, which reported to Markos.[39] For most operations, the Democratic Army still fought at the company and battalion levels. Only for major operations would these separated units combine. The dispersion helped control more territory and was closer to a "traditional" guerrilla disposition, but it meant that senior officers had little experience maneuvering large formations during the few combined operations.[40]

External support was critical to the development of the Democratic Army. Yugoslavia, Bulgaria, and Albania all provided direct support while other communist countries, including the Soviet Union, provided moral support or carefully concealed and limited material support. The United Nations' Balkan Commission documented evidence of all three countries providing sanctuary, transportation, protection, training, weapons, supplies, and medical aid.[41] An example of Yugoslav lethal support was artillery that enabled the Democratic army to shell Salonika for months during the autumn and winter of 1947.[42] A 25 December 1947 meeting of the international communist organization decided to authorize the formal creation of a Free Government of Greece, to be located in Yugoslavia. The meeting decided that all communist countries except the Soviet Union would recognize the new government within three months. Additionally, Yugoslavia and the Soviet Union pledged to provide additional military aid. The Yugoslav representative pledged seventy light tanks, sixty armored cars, and an unspecified number of volunteer units.[43] The Democratic Army was disappointed in the level of support from Moscow. Stalin provided morale and propaganda support, but refrained from actions that could incur international opprobrium for expanding past their sphere of influence.[44]

The Democratic Army had plenty of weapons and frequently had enough food, fodder, fuel, ammunition, and other classes of supply. By

January 1948, the insurgents had enough small arms for their growing force. They also had mortars, artillery, anti-aircraft artillery, bazookas, mines, and machine guns in sufficient quantities.[45] The insurgent logisticians' main problem was delivering the supplies to the widely dispersed fighters. The logistical demands increased as they transformed into a conventional military.[46]

Expanding Control

While the Democratic Army experienced difficulties in transforming its guerrilla units into a conventional military, it was successful in expanding its control over northern Greece and parts of south. This expansion had proceeded so far by September 1947 that the communists had effective control over most of the northern half of Greece except for a handful of cities. Communist influence extended beyond the rural villages. In the cities, the KKE adopted a policy of attacking the ability of the Greek government to rebuild the economy.[47] Senior KKE political leaders operated in Athens by October 1947. There they had sources close to the senior leaders of the Greek government, supported sabotage operations, and attempted to infiltrate social groups, especially labor unions.[48]

Several tactics enabled the Democratic Army to secure large areas and deny it to all but the largest nationalist offensives. First, the continued attacks on small units led the nationalist army and the gendarmerie to withdraw from many locations. In some cases the government had attempted to arm civilians, but these efforts usually failed because lightly armed civilians could not withstand a communist attack without military support. Second, the guerrillas mounted sustained attacks on the infrastructure, which effectively isolated large portions of Greece from government road and rail traffic. Third, the communist auxiliaries and counterintelligence organizations were gaining control of the population in areas abandoned by the government. Guerrilla attacks on railroads, roads, and villages in Thrace in northeastern Greece, brought the situation to the point of crisis. The constant attacks forced the nationalist security forces to abandon all positions along the Bulgarian border and pull out of the villages.[49] This communist progress was a dire threat to the integrity of Greece and called into question the ability of the Greek military to defeat the "bandits" as the military referred to the insurgents.

The Material Situation

In March 1947, the Greek economy was essentially in as bad a situation as it had been in 1944 at the end of the German occupation, despite two years of British and United National relief aid.[50] AMAG took a comprehensive view of the requirements for rebuilding the Greek economy. The overall mission, under the leadership of the State Department, provided assistance to almost every aspect of economic and political life in Greece. The US Army Group--Greece (USAGG), subordinate to the AMAG, provided massive amounts of aid directly to the nationalist army. A third major initiative was the creation of the National Defense Corps to increase the number of forces combating the communist insurgents. These three major programs made a significant contribution to the Greek war effort, but the situation after a year of these efforts was still bleak, leading to the conclusion that economic aid could not defeat the insurgents.

Rebuilding the Economy

The AMAG provided assistance to almost every part of the Greek government under eleven different programs ranging from reconstruction to labor relations. AMAG saw this economic reconstruction as the crucial element in bolstering the nationalists against the communist threat. A brief survey of the various AMAG projects can convey the scope of the US economic aid program. The AMAG reconstruction priorities were roads, bridges, tunnels, railroads, ports, the Corinth Canal, flood control and irrigation. Other programs sought to improve agriculture, industry, mining, exports, and public health.[51] To improve governance, AMAG brought in lawyers and accountants to revise the tax code, change Greek accounting procedures, reform banking laws and reform foreign exchange and credit markets. Advisors also assisted in creating new laws and systems for health, civil service, social security, labor relations, public works, hygiene, and several other areas. The mission directly purchased and distributed food items that were in short supply, provided reconstruction materials, and supervised vaccination programs. The American mission worked with the Greek government to develop an eighteen-month budget that attempted to balance revenues and expenditures.[52]

However, the continued poor security situation mitigated these positive economic results. Guerrilla activity on the roads prevented supplies from reaching much of the rural population. The guerillas captured or destroyed much of the material purchased with the economic reconstruction funds.[53] Additionally, the continued conflict led to tens of thousands of new refugees. By the end of 1947, there were 430,000 refugees, mostly in government-operated camps. In the first quarter of 1948, there were an additional 87,000 refugees. These refugees drained the government coffers, absorbed a significant amount of government administrative capacity, and reduced the total capacity of the economy by removing hundreds of thousands from the workforce.[54] An assessment by AMAG officials in July 1947 concluded that the security situation was so bad that "unless the guerrilla warfare is eliminated or greatly reduced, little progress can be made in the reconstruction of Greece."[55] Consequently, on 6 January 1948, the State Department advised AMAG that "destruction of the guerrilla forces" was of "paramount importance," meaning that military programs would have priority over economic and reconstruction aid.[56] AMAG would first focus on countering the guerrillas and then on improving governance and addressing the root causes of the insurgency.

Sustaining the Greek Military

The War Department, under the auspices of Public Law 75, create the United States Army Group-Greece on 14 April 1947. The USAGG was subordinate to the AMAG and initially had seventeen officers, two soldiers, and twenty-five civilian personnel under the command of Major General William G. Livesay. Livesay had both combat and logistics experience. He commanded the 91st Division commander in the European Theater during World War II and had served as a lieutenant and captain in World War I.[57] After returning from Europe, he commanded a logistics unit and a mobilization unit.[58] The War Department restricted USAGG's mission to only supply matters, believing that the mission could be "effective simply by furnishing the Greek armed forces with what supplies and equipment they needed for the conduct of successful operations against the guerrillas." Additionally, the army wanted to avoid the perception of conducting military operations in Greece.[59] These restrictions meant that only the British provided training to the Greek military. The British Military Mission, which had a smaller presence after 31 March 1947 retained responsibility for overseeing basic training.[60]

Soon after arriving in Greece, however, the US officers began requesting additional authority because the original instructions did not give them enough flexibility to achieve their mission. On 4 June 1947, Ambassador MacVeagh forwarded a USAGG request with his endorsement for the USAGG commander to attend meetings of the High Military Council.[61] This still limited USAGG's influence since it did not yet have authority to attend the Supreme National Defense Council, the equivalent of the US National Security Council.

The Greek government agreed to significant US control over the Greek budget. AMAG had to approve all ministerial budgets and the USAGG had approval authority over the size, organization, and budget of the Greek security forces. The Greek military budget, not including the US contributions, was 584.5 billion drachma, or 44 million dollars.[62] This meant that in dollars the US aid package was paying for two thirds of the Greek military expenditures. Under US pressure to balance the budget, the Greek military made a 24 percent cut.[63] These cuts came despite Greek requests to expand the military and were a reflection of AMAG's priority of making the Greek security forces sustainable by the Greek economy.

The USAGG oversaw a total of 171,850,000 dollars of military aid from March to December 1947. This included 40 million dollars of transferred material and 74 million dollars of purchased material. Some of the procurement included four 500-bed hospitals, 6,500 trucks, 70,000 rifles, and 75 combat and cargo aircraft.[64] USAGG's quartermaster section was responsible for feeding all Greek servicemen, including the army, air force, navy, gendarmerie, and police. The USAGG also provided for the sustenance of the 7,000 "category c" personnel. They were soldiers who had been inducted into the army, but then kept in camps on an island because of suspected communist sympathies.[65]

The USAGG faced continual difficulties in providing enough support to keep the Greek military operational. In the winter 1947-1948, a failure of supply supervision in the Greek air force resulted in a total loss of all winter weight lubricants for the aircraft, requiring the USAGG to make emergency procurement and transportation to enable the planes to resume operations. The nationalist army chose to put hundreds of the American provided supply trucks into storage, even though they could have alleviated the some of the crippling supply problems for units in the field. The Greek officers chose to store these new trucks because they did not have a stockpile of spare parts even though each of the operational corps had only eight or nine trucks for sustainment. The ordnance section of the USAGG formed maintenance inspection teams once it realized that the Greek military was not conducting routine maintenance its of weapons and vehicles. Poor animal treatment, a dearth of veterinary supplies, and ignorance of pack-animal techniques resulted in some mule units, which were essential for mountain operations, being reduced by 50 percent.[66]

Because it was providing most of the funding for the Greek military the United States government had de facto control over the size of Greek military after 31 March 1947. AMAG's initial position was to not increase the size of the nationalist army, even though the British Ambassador to Greece delivered a report to Ambassador MacVeagh on 24 February 1947 that contended that the Greek Army had to be expanded beyond its current 100,000-man ceiling and reorganized if it was to be able to attack the guerrillas.[67] The Truman administration would eventually authorize several increases in the size of the nationalist army during 1947. The administration changed its policy because it recognized that the nationalist army was not able to defeat the communists at its 100,000 man size. The nationalists' military failures convinced Livesay in August 1947 to support the increases even though he had been arguing that the Greek army was large enough. He changed his position because he came to believe that the Greek officers would not be able to use efficiently the men they had, so they would need extra manpower.[68] The Truman administration authorized several increases that brought the permanent size of the GNA to 132,000 in December 1947.[69] A temporary authorized personnel overage put the GNA strength to 142,000 in January 1947.

The Greek General Staff organized its forces into three field divisions, five mountain divisions, three independent brigades, and seven military districts. All of these units reported to one of three corps headquarters. A Corps reported directly to the General Staff while B and C Crops were subordinate to the First Army. There were also 24 commando companies that made up the Raiding Force Headquarters, a separate unit that reported to the First Army.[70]

The Royal Hellenic Air Force (RHAF) had expanded with the help of US procurement to three Spitfire equipped fighter squadrons, one reconnaissance squadron flying Harvards and Austeres, and a transport squadron flying C-47s and Ansons.[71] Livesay and the other US officers would repeatedly push for increased RHAF funding because of their demonstrated aid in attriting the guerrillas. Some estimates indicated that the RHAF accounted for most of the communist casualties.[72]

Partially because of its rapid growth, the military had numerous personnel problems. Many young men, especially those in rural areas, were able to evade the draft because the government officials frequently lacked the transportation to travel to many areas to enforce the draft. These rural soldiers, being familiar with life in the mountains would have been more valuable than city-dwellers. Moreover, politicians frequently interfered to prevent the army from drafting sons from well-connected families. This contributed to an overall shortage of educated soldiers to fill technical specialties. The army responded by increasing the time of service for educated soldiers, which reinforced the incentive for families to use their connections to avoid the draft.[73]

Even with the manpower increases, the army lost territory to the communists, especially after September 1947. This was partially because most of the nationalist army spent their time in static defensive positions, which enabled the guerrillas, at an estimated strength of 22,000 in January

1948, to maneuver relatively unmolested.[74] The Greek General Staff's solution to the nationalists' inability to defend all of the vulnerable areas was to arm civilians on a wider scale than in the past so that these militias could assume the static positions, freeing the army to pursue the insurgents.

Creating the National Defense Corps

The nationalist army had been arming civilians on an informal basis for years to increase the total number of counterinsurgents. The GNA was inconsistent in the level of support it gave to these civilian units. The USAGG sought to have the army formalize this process by creating self-defense units for defensive missions with identified leaders and accountability. The Greek military's initial budget for 1947 included provisions for 5,000 men in Civilian Self-Security Units.[75] Beginning in June, they began lobbying Livesay for funding to expand these militia units. Livesay endorsed this request on 26 June 1947.[76] The final authorization came in September 1947, when the USAGG and the Greek General Staff agreed to organize twenty battalions of 500 men each into a new National Defense Corps (NDC). The military recruited men who had already completed their national service or had been ineligible for the draft to man the new units, in which the men would guard their own villages. The intent of these units was to free the army from static defense operations, so that it could conduct offensive operations against the guerrillas. Although the Greek government had authorized a budget to equip these battalions, that money never materialized, leaving the USAGG with the responsibility of arming the new units. USAGG did so, and used already allocated funds to field forty-two battalions in 1947.[77]

Within months it was clear that even these forty-two battalions would not be enough to enable the nationalist army to go on the offensive. Livesay made this conclusion in December 1947, recommending that the US government authorize 100 battalions.[78] The Truman administration allocated the funds to raise the additional fifty-eight battalions to bring the total to 100 NDC battalions with 50,000 men. Many of the men inducted into the NDC were World War II veterans and knew the terrain and people of their villages intimately, giving them an important advantage in countering the communist insurgency.[79] However, in large part these NDC battalions were not making the GNA more mobile because the GNA established these new militia units in areas where there were no nationalist troops. Consequently, few army garrisons were relieved, and the army expected the paramilitary NDC to fight on their own without support or supervision from army units.[80] The lack of supervision and support from the Greek army for the NDC meant that NDC performance was inconsistent at best. The communists were frequently able to take government-provided weapons away from the paramilitary units that were not supported by regular army units in close proximity.[81] The failures of the NDC were one more in a series of ineffective government attempts to defeat communists.

The Greek National Army and the US Advisors

The security situation deteriorated despite nationalist attempts to defeat the insurgents and the massive influx of US aid. In September 1947, there was a sense of crisis as the communists gained control of large portions of northern Greece. This crisis led to an US decision to increase its focus on military aid and provide operational advice to the Greek military. The Truman administration provided for a new advisory group to address a critical weakness in the Greek military—leadership.

Unsuccessful Battles

By August 1947, the aggressive willingness of the communists to risk close combat had "caught the GNA off balance."[82] The Greek General Staff responded by ordering a series of operations to clear insurgent strongholds in the northern mountains and in the Peloponnese. The first operation, on 14 August 1947 by thirteen battalions attempted to destroy the guerrillas in the Grammos mountains area, a long-time communist stronghold. A communist counterattack stalled the offensive and led the nationalist army to withdraw on 22 August because their soldiers were exhausted. The GNA quickly followed with another operation, this time targeting the mountains near the Yugoslav and Bulgarian borders. The month-long, sixteen-battalion operation failed to engage the guerrillas who were able to evade the slow moving government troops.[83]

In October, the GNA began an operation to trap a guerrilla force of 1,500 men in northwestern Greece near Epirus. The nationalist troops moved faster than normal and threatened to encircle the communist forces. To prevent this, a second Democratic Army unit seized Motsovon on 19 October, a pass on the only road connecting Epirus with the rest of Greece. It took the Greek military until 30 October to retake Epirus, by which time all of the communist soldiers had evacuated the area to a new line along the Grammos Mountains. The nationalist army continued to press the attack, but the communists broke through the nationalists' lines again on 25 November. The GNA chose not to pursue.[84]

While the GNA executed these operations, the Democratic Army unveiled its new artillery during a raid on the town of Pendelefon and expanded its operations in southern Greece in the Peloponnese. In November 1947, the Greek Foreign Minister told Ambassador Dwight

Griswold that the Greek government considered the road from Athens to the Peloponnese cut by guerrilla activity.[85] The General Staff ordered the army to clear the Peloponnese, which the army attempted for three weeks. The operation inconvenienced the guerrillas, but failed to bring them to battle or improve the security on the roads.[86]

The guerrillas continued to demonstrate their strength by attacking Konitsa for a second time on 24 December 1947. Approximately 3,500 guerrillas maintained their attack on the nationalist garrison, the VII Division, which had been reinforced after the July 1947 communist seizure of Konitsa. The nationalists inflicted heavy casualties, but only because the communists continued to assault their positions for two weeks before withdrawing. A simultaneous wave of attacks by communist saboteurs in the major cities contributed to a sense of defeat. In the wake of these battles, the Greek General Staff did not plan any operations for the rest of the winter or the following spring.[87]

There were some positive aspects to the Greek military performance in 1947. One bright spot was the increasing effectiveness of the RHAF. By October 1947, they were flying 570 sorties a month and responsible for the majority of the casualties. Nevertheless, the Democratic Army was able to retain the initiative. The "Government forces did not participate in a single major engagement that they were not forced into by initial guerrilla action."[88] The Greek soldiers were courageous when "forced into skirmishes," but their commanders were often "reluctant to order their men to destroy surrounded guerrillas or to pursue guerrilla units which had commenced to withdraw."[89] As a result, the Democratic Army had the freedom to conduct operations across most of Greece. By December 1947, the situation had deteriorated to the point that the State Department and National Security Council considered the deployment of up to a corps from the US Army to control Greece's northern border or secure the main cities.[90]

The Greek army's official explanations for its failure to defeat the guerrillas centered on reasons why it could not carry the fight into the mountains. They did not have enough machine guns or artillery, and they had not yet have sufficient security in the cities. One US observer in the mission, John Coppock, noted that the Greek General Staff had an interest in keeping US military forces in Greece as a deterrent against aggression from their northern neighbors. Consequently, at least some officers did not want to defeat the insurgency completely. They were unwilling to undertake an aggressive campaign against the insurgent strongholds in the mountains.[91]

The US assessment at the end of 1947 concluded that guerrilla groups maintained the initiative and in their fighting against government forces were able to participate in decisive combat or avoid it as they chose. Rebel groups were able to move freely over large portions of Greece and could infiltrate through Greek Army lines and concentrate in other areas. Over wide areas, the guerrillas terrorized the populace by savage raids against villages and by acts of sabotage against government installations. For short periods, the guerrillas were able to control extensive stretches of territory.[92]

The Greek government, the senior Americans in Greece, and the Truman administration had all concluded that US material and moral support would not be sufficient to defeat the communist threat. Until the Greek security forces could isolate areas from communist influence, AMAG and the Greek government could not govern or address the population's grievances. Individuals in these organizations had been working toward this consensus since August 1947.

The Decision to Provide Operational Advice

In August 1947, the USAGG recognized that an expanded training and supply mission would not be sufficient to field an effective Greek army. An intelligence summary of the US reports from Greece indicated that the situation in Greece was precarious and that the nationalist army was unable to defeat the guerrillas.[93] Based on his observations of Greek operations, Livesay concluded that Greek officers were not aggressive enough and did not know how to prepare and use their men. In a 31 August 1947 meeting of the Supreme National Defense Council, Livesay brought up several criticisms of the GNA. He stated that the Greek officers were not preparing their soldiers for operations, citing the fact that most operations rapidly culminated because the soldiers' feet were too sore to continue. Additionally, the General Staff was not managing its units so that there could be a rotation to allow units to rest and conduct training while other units pursued the guerrillas.[94] Livesay reiterated his criticism of Greek commanders on 6 October 1947 by recommending that the Minister of War relieve the C Corps commander for a lack of diligence and aggressiveness. This commander, Major General Papageorgios, had consistently failed to see his units in the field and issued orders prohibiting patrols in less than company strength, an order that would dramatically reduce the chance of finding the enemy. Livesay also recommended the relief of the most senior officer, the Chief of the General Staff for not cooperating with the Prime Minister. The Minister of War did not follow these recommendations.[95]

The US advisors would find many examples of Greek officers who did not want to take aggressive action or did not know how to command their forces effectively. A battalion commander in Salonika did not even consider sending infantry to attack a communist artillery position, preferring to attempt to suppress it with his own mortars.[96] Greek officers preferred "fighting at long range," resulting in an inability to compel the guerrillas into positions where the GNA could destroy them.[97] Greek commanders would frequently use a technique that the Americans dubbed the "double-company." A brigade commander would assign an objective to two companies from two different battalions under the command of an officer from a third battalion. The result was that everyone ended up waiting for the other units. This situation suited all of the officers since they all had ready excuses for their failure to find the enemy--they could always blame the other battalions.[98]

The USAGG officers recognized that it would have to expand its operations beyond the War Department restrictions, up to the full extent authorized by Public Law 75.[99] On 15 September 1947, Griswold sent an urgent cable to the Secretary of State, George C. Marshall about the deteriorating situation and his recommendations. Based on the conclusions of his staff and Livesay, he averred that the United States should deploy 150-200 officers to provide operational advice to the Greek General Staff and tactical units. Griswold argued that "an offensive spirit and [the] benefit of tactical advice to eliminate continued ineffective military operations which play directly into communist hands."[100] Based on the urgency of the situation, Griswold also recommended transferring six million dollars from the reconstruction accounts to military aid, continuing a temporary 20 thousand man increase in the size of the nationalist army, and funding a permanent 10 thousand man increase.[101]

Within four days of receiving this cable, the Chief of Staff of the Army sent the Army G-2, Director of Intelligence, Major General Stephen Chamberlin, to Greece to assess the situation before the Army agreed to support Griswold and Livesay's requests.[102] Chamberlin delivered his exhaustive report on 20 October 1947. This report agreed with the assessment of Livesay, Griswold and other US observers. The root of the problem was in declining soldier quality, poor officer combat leadership, lack of senior officer offensive spirit, poor unit training, and a lack of cooperation. To remedy these problems, he recommended expanding the NDC, US operational advice to the senior leaders, and US observers with tactical units.[103] Chamberlin's report coincided with an official request from the Greek government for operational advice. President Truman agreed to expand operational advice down to the division level on 11 November 1947.[104] The Joint Chiefs of Staff initiated a study of the Chamberlin Report, which resulted in new directives on 11 December 1947 on how to organize the new advisory organization.[105]

Creation of the JUSMAPG

On 31 December 1947, the Joint Chiefs of Staff created the Joint United States Military Advisory and Planning Group-Greece (JUSMAPG). This organization reported to the Joint Chiefs of Staff and the Chief of AMAG. Both AMAG and JUSMAPG had command authority over USAGG, which continued to execute the sustainment mission.[106] The USAGG in turn reported to the Army staff, not to the Joint Chiefs as the JUSMAPG did. Initially only AMAG had authority over the United States Naval Group-Greece, but JUSMAPG had its own naval section to advise the Greek Royal Navy. It would take over a year before the leaders in Greece were able to streamline this confusing organization.[107]

The Joint Chiefs gave Livesay command of both JUSMAPG and USAGG.[108] He immediately began to build the new advisory organization as the 170 (90 officers and 80 soldiers) newly assigned personnel began arriving in Greece in December and January. Livesay had two criteria for the officer advisors: graduation of the Command and General Staff College and combat experience.[109] He created four sections to advise the Greek General Staff on personnel, intelligence, operations, and logistics. These General Staff advisors and Livesay, as the chief advisor and member of the Supreme National Defense Council, had five tasks: monitoring the military situation, "formulate plans for the employment and coordination of the Armed Forces of Greece," advise the Joint Chiefs and the Chief of AMAG on how to use the Greek military, provide operational advice, and ensure that "operational returns are commensurate with the aid furnished."[110] The wording of the second and fifth tasks clearly indicates that Livesay and JUSMAPG intended to have a significant level of influence over Greek military operations.

To provide operational advice and monitoring of GNA operations, Livesay created eleven field teams to advise the First Army, the three corps, and the seven divisions of the GNA. These teams and the General Staff advisors spent six weeks until the end of February assessing the GNA. The product of this assessment was a plan with the objective of ending the war in 1948. To accomplish this ambitious goal, JUSMAPG requested to expand the nationalist army another 13.6 percent to 150,000 men.[111] The Truman administration denied this request for budget reasons, although it would approve on 27 March a subsequent request to fund a 15,000 man temporary personnel overage for six months.

These new US advisors, combat veterans of World War II, did not confine themselves to only assessing the Greek military. Livesay's instructions to the new advisors included this guidance: "you must insist on aggressive action . . . we must instill aggressiveness in them; they must carry the fight to the bandits."[112] From the beginning of his command in Greece, Livesay had been emphasizing aggressiveness. In July, he relieved two colonels for a lack of aggressiveness, even though they were ordnance specialists and technical experts.[113] While these advisors were positioned at the general staff, corps, and division levels, Livesay instructed them to "maintain close personal contact with lower echelons . . . to insure aggressive action."[114]

The emphasis on aggressiveness soon resulted in reports of US officers commanding Greek units in combat. On 10 February 1948, Democratic Army units shelled the city of Salonika.[115] The Greek Navy and Air Force responded by attacking suspected communist positions with bombs and naval gunfire.[116] Additionally, local GNA units encountered communist units. A United Press journalist reported that Colonel Regnier, a division level advisor, led a platoon assault up a hill to seize a communist position. Since Public Law 75 prohibited US personnel from commanding Greek units, this story started a significant fracas.[117] However, the subsequent actions of Livesay and the officers in the Plans and Operations Division of the Department of the Army indicate that they did not want to hinder aggressive US officers who were pushing Greek units to close with and destroy communist units. The investigation consisted of an interview with Regnier and the journalist, which satisfied the investigating officer that Regnier was only advising and that the journalist had relied on Greek sources, having not seen the battle himself.[118] The command submitted a memorandum by Regnier stating that he had been advising a Greek major who "seemed to be helpless in the situation."[119] With this documentation, the Army considered the issue closed. As long as the US officers could write a memorandum stating that they were advising, the chain of command would not restrict them, even if it was a veteran infantry colonel advising a Greek lieutenant from the center of the lieutenant's formation during a battle. Aggressive US officers would still be able to have significant influence over tactical operations. At this same time, the US advisors were in the process of gaining more influence over the entire Greek chain of command from platoon level to the Greek General Staff.

Greek Leadership

The Truman administration based its decision to provide operational advice on the evolving US recognition that leadership failures were a primary cause of the GNA's ineffectiveness against the communists. The advisors to the General Staff quickly realized that "the Chief of Staff had little authority over his subordinate commanders, orders from the [Greek General Staff] were often ignored by lower commanders, [and] cabinet members and other politicians gave orders to commanders in the field, completely disregarding the army command structure."[120] While the General staff had minimal ability to control operational aspects, it attempted to micromanage every administrative detail. On one occasion, the General Staff spent two hours debating the promotion of one lieutenant.[121]

Throughout the Greek military, the US advisors saw a general passive defensive mindset and a lack of initiative. Livesay summarized these observations in a briefing to the Chairman of the Joint Chiefs, General Omar Bradley. Among his nineteen points, he stated that "officers are afraid to take the initiative;" there is a "disinclination to come to grips with the bandits and a lack of offensive spirit;" and, officers feel that there "is no determined political leadership." RHAF commanders had given their pilots orders to "fly sorties only on demand from the army and then as few as possible."[122] The US officers believed that this poor leadership from platoon to cabinet level was defeating the nationalist cause.

On 31 January 1948, the Greek cabinet ordered changes in the military organization that sought to minimize US and British influence and prevent the rise of a single powerful general. The changes abolished the First Army, resulting in all three corps reporting to the General Staff. It also moved operational decisions from the High Military Council, over which the US advisors had developed significant influence, to the Supreme National Defense Council. The two US representatives, Livesay and Griswold, both sat on this council, but could not vote, a fact that limited their influence on contested issues. Cabinet members began bypassing the Greek Chief of Staff and even corps commanders to give orders directly to battalions in the field.[123]

On 14 February 1948, in response to this maneuver by the Greek cabinet, officials representing the British and US ambassadors met with the Prime Minister and his cabinet. They delivered a letter demanding increased independence for the GNA Chief of Staff and specified roles for the US and British advisors. Centralizing control of the military under the Chief of Staff was a means of limiting political micromanagement and leaks about operations to the communists that were decreasing military effectiveness.[124] The letter had an attached agreement that required the Greek government to acknowledge the authority of the US advisors. While it stated that they were only advising not commanding, the agreement required the Greek government to consult with the US and British advisors on every decision that affected the military. This included "all questions of command, organization and training, the strategy and tactics of the anti-guerrilla campaign, all plans of contemplated operations, all laws and decrees affecting the army, and all appointments or promotions to the rank of brigadier or higher."[125] The agreement also listed an appeal process if a Greek official disagreed with the US advice. This process was to refer the question to the Prime Minister who had to consult the AMAG Chief, US Ambassador, and the British Ambassador before making a decision. The requirement would have made it clear to any Greek officer that he would have to listen to US advice since the Americans had just demonstrated that they had significant negotiating strength over the Prime Minister.

The Greek government agreed with the Americans, and issued the necessary orders on 19 February 1948 to implement the new agreement.[126] The JUSMAPG General Staff advisors immediately began pushing the plans officers in the Greek General Staff to plan a major offensive to clear the Roumeli of all guerrilla activity. As a measure of the Americans' new influence, they were able to overcome resistance from the Greek officers who did not want to dedicate three divisions to the Roumeli operation because that would have meant accepting risk somewhere else. The General Staff also acceded to the US suggestions to establish mobile reserve forces in each of the major regions so that they could counter guerrilla operations. The Greek General Staff had opposed both of these recommendations because they preferred to keep as many troops as possible in static positions, as they had been doing for the whole war.[127]

Summary

The continued communist successes during 1947 demonstrated to the US advisors and the Truman administration that the critical weakness of nationalist government was the GNA's combat leadership. The conclusion led to the decision to extend operational advice. It also led the US advisors to conclude that they had to find a way to instill aggressiveness in the nationalist military. The advisors continued their focus on aggressiveness, even if imparting aggressiveness to their Greek counterparts required the advisors to enter combat or attempt to control the GNA. The next major change came on 24 February when Major General James Van Fleet assumed command of JUSMAPG.[128] The arrival of a new US commander, the increased US influence, and the planned spring 1948 offensives marked the beginning of a new phase in the Greek Civil War.

Notes

1. John L. Gaddis, *Strategies of Containment* (Oxford: Oxford University Press, 1982), 13-17.

2. Gaddis, 19.

3. George Kennan, Telegram from George Kennan to George Marshall, 22 February 1946, President Harry S. Truman Library, http://www.trumanlibrary.org/
whistlestop/study_collections/coldwar/documents/pdf/6-6.pdf (accessed 25 August 2012); George Kennan, "The Sources of Soviet Conduct," *Foreign Affairs* 25, no. 4 (July 1947): 566-582.

4. Kennan, 17.

5. Jones, 7-10.

6. Jones, 11-13.

7. Lawrence S. Wittner, *American Intervention in Greece, 1943-1949* (New York: Columbia University Press, 1982), 56-57.

8. Jones, 5.

9. Intelligence Division, "Soviet Intransigence in the Greek Border Investigation," *Intelligence Review*, no. 79 (21 August 1947): 23-31. Archives, Military History Institute, Carlisle Barracks, PA.

10. Mark Ethridge, Telegram to the Secretary of State, 17 February 1947, *Foreign Relations of the United States, 1947, The Near East and Africa*, http://digital.library.
wisc.edu/1711.dl/FRUS, 830 (accessed 10 October 2012).

11. However, there was increasing friction between Yugoslavia and the Soviet Union that had begun in 1946. This friction would lead to an open split that harmed the KKE. See John Swissler, "The Transformations of American Cold War Policy Toward Yugoslavia, 1948-1951" (Ph.d diss., University of Hawaii, 1993), 3-17.

12. Wittner, 20-21. The United States was partially concerned about securing access to Middle Eastern oil.

13. Wittner, 50-52, 60; Jones, 24.

14. Department of State, Memorandum for the Secretary of State, "Critical Situation in Greece," 20 February 1947, General Records of the Department of State, Records of the Officer-in-Charge of Greek Affairs, Subject File 1944-1951, Box 39.

15. Department of State.

16. Paul A. Porter, "Report of the American Economic Mission to Greece," Paul A. Porter Papers, President Harry S. Truman Library, Independence, MO, 11a. Conversion to 2012 dollars based on the Consumer Price Index, calculated

using MeasuringWorth.com, "Measuring Worth," www.measuringworth.com (accessed 19 October 2012).

17. Jones, 28-30.

18. Griswold, "Memorandum re Greek Situation," 2.

19. Coppock, "Greece-End of 1948," 4.

20. Dwight P. Griswold, excerpts from letter to the State Department, 14 August 1947, Dwight P. Griswold Papers, Harry S. Truman Presidential Library, Independence MO, Box 1, 2.

21. Paul A. Porter, "American Economic Mission to Greece Diary 22 January 1947," Paul A. Porter Papers, President Harry S. Truman Library, Independence, MO.

22. Public Law 75, http://www.trumanlibrary.org/whistlestop/study_collections/
doctrine/large/documents/index.php?pagenumber=1&documentdate=1947-05-22&documentid=5-2 (accessed 1 October 2012).

23. Dwight P. Griswold, "Memorandum Re Greek Conditions," Dwight P. Griswold Papers, Harry S. Truman Presidential Library, Independence MO, Box 1 AMAG Correspondence, 1; Intelligence Division, "The Military Topography of Greece," *Intelligence Review,* no. 81 (4 September 1947): 30-38, Archives: Military History Institute, Carlisle Barracks, PA.

24. George C. Marshall, letter to Dwight P. Griswold, Dwight P. Griswold Papers, Harry S. Truman Presidential Library, Independence MO, Box 1, 2.

25. Dwight P. Griswold, undated and untitled essay, Dwight P. Griswold Papers, Harry S. Truman Presidential Library, Independence MO, Box 1, 2.

26. Harry S. Truman, "Statement by the President," 5 June 1947, Official File, 426, President Harry S. Truman Library, Independence MO, Box 1426.

27. George C. Marshall, telegram to Paul Porter from George Marshall, 1 March 1947, Paul A. Porter Papers, President Harry S. Truman Library, Independence, MO, 2.

28. Lincoln MacVeagh, telegram to George Marshall from Lincoln MacVeagh, 2 March 1947, Paul A. Porter Papers, President Harry S. Truman Library, Independence, MO, 1-2.

29. Plans and Operations Division, Memorandum for General Wedemeyer, "State Department Views Reference Greek Problem," 29 December 1947, Records of the Army Staff, Plans and Operations Division, National Archives and Records Administration, College Park, MD, Records Group 319, Entry 154, Decimal File 091, Box 13.

30. Shrader, 140.

31. Intelligence Division, "The Military Topography of Greece,"

Intelligence Review, no. 81 (4 September 1947): 30-38, Archives: Military History Institute, Carlisle Barracks, PA.

32. Intelligence Division, "Armed Band Activity in Greece," *Intelligence Review,* no. 50 (30 June 1947): 18-19, Military History Institute, Carlisle Barracks, PA.

33. Intelligence Division, "The Greek Guerrillas-How They Operate," *Intelligence Review*, no. 156 (March 1949): 33, Archives: Military History Institute, Carlisle Barracks, PA.

34. Shrader, 114.

35. US Army, *History of the Joint United States Military Advisory and Planning Group-Greece*, United States Army Unit Dairies, Histories and Reports, Miscellaneous Units, Records Group 407, President Harry S. Truman Library, Independence, MO, 37.

36. George C. Marshall, "Memorandum for the President, Subject: Greek Situation," 16 July 1947, Harry S. Truman Papers, President's Secretary's File, President Harry S. Truman Library, Independence, MO, Box 112, 1-3.

37. Kousoulas, 252-254; Shrader, 65-71.

38. Shrader, 97, 114.

39. US Army, *JUSMAPG*, 17.

40. Shrader, 223.

41. Herbert Evatt, "Committee No. 1 (Political) of the United Nations, Speech of the Australian Foreign Minister on the Greek Question," Harry S. Truman Papers, President's Secretary's File, President Harry S. Truman Library, Independence, MO, Box 157, 6-7.

42. "Quarterly Report on Aid to Greece and Turkey," Official File 426, President Harry S. Truman Library, Independence, MO, Box 1426, 21.

43. It is not clear how much of the pledged aid Yugoslavia actually delivered to the KKE. Department of State, Intelligence Report, date of information 26 December 1947, President's Secretary's File, President Harry S. Truman Library, Independence, MO, Box 112, 1-5; Yugoslav soldiers were enlisted in Greek guerrilla units as part of their service to Yugoslavia: US Army, "Bandit Activity on Yugoslavian-Greek Frontier," 25 August 1947, Army Intelligence Document File, BID 394852, Records Group 319, National Archives and Records Administration, College Park, MD.

44. Shrader, 170. There were unconfirmed reports of Soviet offers to provide jet fighters and Soviet officers in Greek uniform. There is no evidence that these offers materialized into actual aid. For example, see US Army, BID 394852.

45. US Army, "Bandit Weapons in the 588th Battalion," Army Intelligence Document File, BID 494972, Records Group 319, National Archives and Records Administration, College Park, MD.

46. Shrader, 147-148.

47. US Army, "KKE Activities," Army Intelligence Document File, BID 337557, Records Group 319, National Archives and Records Administration, College Park, MD.

48. Department of State, "The Communist Party of Greece," General Records of the Department of State, Records of the Officer-in-Charge of Greek Affairs, Subject File 1944-1951, Box 39.

49. American Embassy, Athens, Greece, Memorandum of Conversation, "Situation in Thrace," 10 September 1947, Records of the Army Staff, Plans and Operations Division, National Archives and Records Administration, College Park, MD, Records Group 319, Entry 154, Decimal File 091, Box 13.

50. John Coppock, "Memo from Greece," John Coppock Papers, President Harry S. Truman Library, Independence, MO, Box 1, 3.

51. Department of State, Letter of Instruction to Dwight Griswold, 12 July 1947, General Records of the Department of State, National Archives and Records Administration, College Park, MD, Records of the Office of Greek, Turkish, and Iranian Affairs, Subject File 1947-1950, Box 1.

52. Harry S. Truman, "Quarterly Report on Aid to Greece and Turkey," President Harry S. Truman Library, Independence, MO, Official File 426, Box 1426, Folder Greece and Turkey 1947, 33, 36-37.

53. William Livesay, Memorandum for Dwight Griswold, "Increase in Strength of the Greek Army," 21 August 1947, General Records of the Department of State, National Archives and Records Administration, College Park, MD, Records of the Officer-in-Charge of Greek Affairs, Subject File 1944-1951, Box 39.

54. Truman, "Quarterly Report on Aid to Greece and Turkey," 35. 2986.

55. Loy Henderson, "Skouras Memorandum," Dwight G. Griswold Papers, Harry S. Truman Presidential Library, Independence, MO, Box 1, 1; Department of State, "Comments on Griswold Report for Month of August," 15 October 1947, General Records of the Department of State, Records of the Officer-in-Charge of Greek Affairs, Subject File 1944-1951, Box 39.

56. Plans and Operations Division, "Future Concept and Objectives of Military Aid for Greece," Records of the Army Staff, Plans and Operations Division, National Archives and Records Administration, College Park, MD, Records Group 319, Entry 153, Decimal File 091, Box 74; US Army, *JUSMAPG*, 46.

57. "World War Veteran Takes Command of Fir Tree Division; Promises Strenuous Action," *Camp White Grenade* 22 July 1943, 1, Archives: William G. Livesay Papers, Military History Institute, Carlisle Barracks, PA.

58. Benjamin Taylor, Memorandum for the Department of State, 12 June

1947, Records of the Army Staff, Plans and Operations Division, National Archives and Records Administration, College Park, MD, Records Group 319, Entry 153, Decimal File 091, Box 74.

59. United States Army Group-Greece, *History of the Joint United States Army Group-Greece*, United States Army Unit Dairies, Histories and Reports, Miscellaneous Units, Records Group 407, President Harry S. Truman Library, Independence, MO, 75-76; Colonel Lehner, Cable to War Department Plans and Operations, 14 June 1947, Records of Interservice Organizations, Joint United States Military Advisory Group Greece, Records Group 334, Entry 146, Incoming and Outgoing Messages, Box 112.

60. Intelligence Division, "Capabilities of the Greek National Army," *Intelligence Review,* no. 96 (18 December 1947): 50, Archives: Military History Institute, Carlisle Barracks, PA.

61. Lincoln MacVeagh, Message for the Secretary of State, 4 June 1947, Records of the Army Staff, Plans and Operations Division, National Archives and Records Administration, College Park, MD, Records Group 319, Entry 153, Decimal File 091, Box 74.

62. The author converted the drachma into a dollar sum using an estimate of actual market exchange rate (as opposed to the official rate or purchasing power parity) for February 1948. The rate was 13,000 drachmas for one dollar. Exchange rate reported in: American Mission for Aid to Greece, Monthly Report of the Chief of AMAG to the Secretary of State, 15 April 1948, General Records of the Department of State, National Archives and Records Administration, College Park, MD, Records Group 59, Records of the Office of Greek, Turkish, and Iranian Affairs, Subject File, Greece-Turkey 1947-1950, Box 21, 12.

63. United States Army Group-Greece, *History of the Joint United States Army Group-Greece Vol II*, United States Army Unit Dairies, Histories and Reports, Miscellaneous Units, Records Group 407, President Harry S. Truman Library, Independence, MO, 29.

64. US Army, *USAGG Vol II,* 13, 44, 57-58, 95.

65. US Army, 97-98.

66. US Army, 16, 42, 49, 73-76, 97-98.

67. Lincoln MacVeagh, telegraph 27 February 1947, Paul A. Porter Papers, President Harry S. Truman Library, Independence MO, 1-4.

68. William Livesay, Memorandum for Dwight Griswold, "Increase in Strength of the Greek Army," 21 August 1947, General Records of the Department of State, National Archives and Records Administration, College Park, MD, Records of the Officer-in-Charge of Greek Affairs, Subject File 1944-1951, Box 39.

69. US Army, *USAGG Vol II*, 14.

70. US Army, *JUSMAPG*, 47.

71. US Army, 48.

72. William Livesay, Cable dated 29 August 1947, Records of Interservice Organizations, Joint United States Military Advisory Group Greece, Records Group 334, Entry 146, Incoming and Outgoing Messages, Box 112, 3.

73. US Army, *JUSMAPG*, 23.

74. US Army, 47.

75. US Army, *USAGG Vol II*, 30, 40.

76. William Livesay, Cable to Dwight Griswold, 26 June 1947, Records of Interservice Organizations, Joint United States Military Advisory Group Greece, Records Group 334, Entry 146, Incoming and Outgoing Messages, Box 112.

77. US Army, *JUSMAPG*, 29.

78. US Army.

79. E. J. C. Hare, "Report of Field Trip to Lamia," 8 December 1947, General Records of the Department of State, Records of the Office of Greek, Turkish, and Iranian Affairs, Subject File 1947-1950, Box 14; US Army, *USAGG Vol II*, 14.

80. US Army, *JUSMAPG*, 48.

81. United States Army Group Greece, "Minutes of Meeting Held in General Livesay's Office," 12 September 1947, Records of the Army Staff, Plans and Operations Division, National Archives and Records Administration, College Park, MD, Records Group 319, Entry 153, Decimal File 091, Box 77.

82. US Army, *JUSMAPG*, 37.

83. US Army, 37-38.

84. US Army, 38-39.

85. American Mission for Aid to Greece, Telegram for the Secretary of State, 29 November 1947, Harry S. Truman Papers, President's Secretary's Files, President Harry S. Truman Library, Independence, MO, Box 112, 2.

86. US Army, *JUSMAPG*, 39.

87. US Army, 16, 39, 47.

88. US Army, 40.

89. John O. Coppock, "Greece," John O. Coppock Papers, President Harry S. Truman Library, Independence, MO, 4-5; US Army, *JUSMAPG*, 40.

90. Department of State, Memorandum of Conversation, "Greek Situation," General Records of the Department of State, Records of the Officer-in-Charge of Greek Affairs, Subject File 1944-1951, National Archives and Records Administration, College Park, MD, Box 39; Department of State,

"Function of Foreign Troops in Greece," 12 January 1948, General Records of the Department of State, National Archives and Records Administration, College Park, MD, Records of the Officer-in-Charge of Greek Affairs, Subject File 1944-1951, Box 39.

91. Coppock, "Greece," 18.

92. US Army, *JUSMAPG*, 19.

93. Intelligence Division, "The Military Situation in Greece," *Intelligence Review,* no. 77 (7 August 1947): 37-42, Archives: Military History Institute, Carlisle Barracks, PA.

94. William Livesay, Diary, 31 August 1947, William Livesay Papers, Military History Institute, Carlisle Barracks, PA. Livesay had apparently become more aggressive in his criticisms of leadership failures during August. His diary for the beginning of the month gives the impression that he was fairly passive during meetings, even when the discussion turned to the relief of general officers, for example see the entry for 4 August 1947.

95. William Livesay, Diary, 6 October 1947, William Livesay Papers, Military History Institute, Carlisle Barracks, PA.

96. William Livesay, untitled speech, 16 January 1948, William Livesay Papers, Military History Institute, Carlisle Barracks, PA, 4.

97. Department of State, Memorandum of Conversation, "Greek Situation," General Records of the Department of State, Records of the Officer-in-Charge of Greek Affairs, Subject File 1944-1951, Box 39.

98. James A. Van Fleet, "Interview with General James A. Van Fleet by Lieutenant Colonel Bruce Williams," James A. Van Fleet Papers, Military History Institute, Carlisle Barracks, PA, Interview 3, Tape 3, 9.

99. US Army, *USAGG Vol II*, 13.

100. Dwight G. Griswold, "AMAG 222," Dwight P. Griswold Papers, Harry S. Truman Presidential Library, Independence MO, Box 1, 2-3.

101. Griswold, 1-3.

102. Department of State, telegram to Griswold, 19 September 1947, Dwight P. Griswold Papers, Harry S. Truman Presidential Library, Independence MO, Box 1, 1.

103. Stephen Chamberlin, "The Greek Situation: Report to the Chief of Staff," 20 October 1947, Records of the Army Staff, Plans and Operations Division, National Archives and Records Administration, College Park, MD, Records Group 319, Entry 154, Decimal File 091, Box 15, 3.

104. Plans and Operations Division, Note For Record, 14 November 1947, Records of the Army Staff, Plans and Operations Division, National Archives and Records Administration, College Park, MD, Records Group 319, Entry 153, Decimal File 091, Box 74; US Army, *USAGG, Vol II*, 14.

105. Joint Chiefs of Staff, Memorandum for Record, "Joint US Military Advisory and Planning Group in Greece," 11 December 1947, Records of the Army Staff, Plans and Operations Division, National Archives and Records Administration, College Park, MD, Records Group 319, Entry 153, Decimal File 091, Box 14; US Army, *JUSMAPG*, 43.

106. US Army, *JUSMAPG*, 44.

107. US Army, 43-44.

108. War Department, Cable to USAGG, Athens, 6 January 1948, Records of Interservice Organizations, Joint United States Military Advisory Group Greece, National Archives and Records Administration, College Park, MD, Records Group 334, Entry 146, Incoming and Outgoing Messages, Box 92.

109. Plans and Operations Division, Note for Record, "Re-assignment of staff officers to USAGG," Records of the Army Staff, Plans and Operations Division, National Archives and Records Administration, College Park, MD, Records Group 319, Entry 154, Decimal File 091, Box 13.

110. US Army, *JUSMAPG*, 45.

111. William Livesay, Cable to Director Plans and Operations, 22 January 1948, Records of Interservice Organizations, Joint United States Military Advisory Group Greece, National Archives and Records Administration, College Park, MD, Records Group 334, Entry 146, Incoming and Outgoing Messages, Box 113.

112. William Livesay, untitled speech, 16 January 1948, William Livesay Papers, Military History Institute, Carlisle Barracks, PA, 4. This speech is untitled, however, from the date and the instructions given in the speech I infer that it was given to the advisors who had recently arrived during their orientation training.

113. William Livesay, Replacement of Officer Personnel, 14 July 1947, Records of the Army Staff, Plans and Operations Division, National Archives and Records Administration, College Park, MD, Records Group 319, Entry 153, Decimal File 091, Box 74.

114. William Livesay, "Joint US Military Advisory and Planning Group (JUSMAPG)," 15 January 1948, Records of the Army Staff, Plans and Operations Division, National Archives and Records Administration, College Park, MD, Records Group 319, Entry 153, Decimal File 091, Box 75, 4. 5976.

115. The communists' ability to move artillery guns and ammunition into the mountains to conduct this operation indicates an impressive level of organization and will that reflects poorly on the GNA.

116. William Livesay, Love 615, Records of Interservice Organizations, Joint United States Military Advisory Group Greece, National Archives and Records Administration, College Park, MD, Records Group 334, Entry 146, Incoming and Outgoing Messages, Box 113.

117. William Livesay, Cable to Plans and Operations Division, 12 February 1948, Records of Interservice Organizations, Joint United States Military Advisory Group Greece, National Archives and Records Administration, College Park, MD, Records Group 334, Entry 146, Incoming and Outgoing Messages, Box 113.

118. William Livesay, Cable to Plans and Operations Division, 15 February 1948, Records of Interservice Organizations, Joint United States Military Advisory Group Greece, National Archives and Records Administration, College Park, MD, Records Group 334, Entry 146, Incoming and Outgoing Messages, Box 113.

119. A. J. Regnier, "United Press Report," 18 February 1948, Records of the Army Staff, Plans and Operations Division, National Archives and Records Administration, College Park, MD, Records Group 319, Entry 153, Decimal File 000.5 to 000.9, Box 1.

120. US Army, *JUSMAPG*, 54.

121. Hubert R. Gallager, "Administrative Reorganization in the Greek Crisis," *Public Administrative Review* 8, no. 4 (Autumn 1948): 257.

122. William Livesay, "Review of the Military Situation in Greece," William Livesay Papers, Military History Institute, Carlisle Barracks, PA.

123. William Livesay, Cable to Plans and Operations Division, 2 February 1947, Records of Interservice Organizations, Joint United States Military Advisory Group Greece, National Archives and Records Administration, College Park, MD, Records Group 334, Entry 146, Incoming and Outgoing Messages, Box 113; US Army, *JUSMAPG*, 57.

124. James Van Fleet, Cable for General Wedemeyer, 27 February 1947, Records of Interservice Organizations, Joint United States Military Advisory Group Greece, National Archives and Records Administration, College Park, MD, Records Group 334, Entry 146, Incoming and Outgoing Messages, Box 113.

125. US Army, *JUSMAPG*, 57.

126. US Army, 58.

127. US Army, 61.

128. US Army.

Chapter 4
Expansion Of The Advisory Mission And The End Of The War
February 1948-September 1949

Exploitation must repeat must be pushed strongly today repeat today. Waiting will give the bandits chance to regroup and man defensive positions. If situation needs clarifying then clarify it with bold and aggressive attack now; it cannot repeat cannot be clarified by command and staff conferences and observations, nor will bandits clarify it for you. Clarify it with combat troops throwing their weight against demoralized Vitsi bandits with all speed and greatest possible weight.

— Brigadier General Reuben Jenkins, Cable to II Division

Strategic Situation

Throughout 1948 and 1949, the intensification of the Cold War between the Soviet Union and the United States created a sense of urgency for the war in Greece and imposed limitations. The growing number of US commitments around the world in an effort to contain communist expansion increased the drain on limited resources. Moreover, the Truman knew that he could not undermine the domestic economy. The President repeatedly looked to reduce the budget for the various US operations around the world, including the Greek operation. In November 1948, President Truman decided that it had to prioritize the deteriorating situation in China over the aid to Greece and Turkey.[1]

The communist blockade of West Berlin, which began on 24 June 1948, signaled a major escalation in the Cold War and had an immediate effect on the war effort in Greece. Because of the requirements for the Berlin airlift, the US Air Force diverted aircraft, supplies, and parts that had been procured for the RHAF. It also transferred JUSMAPG's aircraft to Germany for the duration of the airlift. The Air Force Group in Greece had to request special procurement authority to buy spare parts for the RHAF or else it could not have kept its aircraft flying after December 1948.[2]

The increasing evidence of communist expansion and subversion around the world led many in the administration and JUSMAPG to conclude that the KKE was acting on orders from Moscow. Van Fleet, for example, argued throughout his life that the Soviet Union was directly controlling the Greek communists.[3] Ironically, the US commitment to Greece had convinced Stalin that the KKE could not achieve a victory in Greece.

Because a dramatic defeat would damage the prestige of international communism, he ordered the insurgency to end. Yugoslavia, Albania, and Bulgaria, however, did not listen and continued to support the KKE and the Democratic Army for their own goals. Soviet and communist propaganda also enthusiastically used every opportunity to embarrass the Greek nationalists and the US government. After the nationalists demonstrated that they might achieve a decisive military victory in the summer of 1949, the Soviet Union began a peace offensive to achieve a truce or at least portray the US and the nationalists as war-mongers. Additionally, the Soviet members of the United Nations' Balkan Commission prevented it from affecting the security of Greece's northern border.[4]

The dynamics of Cold War deterrence also limited US options. The administration knew that pressuring the Balkan Soviet satellites too much risked expanding the conflict.[5] The administration successfully engaged Yugoslavia as it broke from the Soviet bloc. This engagement significantly reduced the Greek communists' supplies. Nevertheless, the administration had limited options for dealing with Albania and Bulgaria. The administration's policy options inside Greece were also limited. The Greek government resisted any reforms that would "infringe upon or inconvenience various entrenched political and economic interests."[6] These entrenched economic interests resisted modernization efforts or changes to Greek macroeconomics. A US official Greece reported that he knew "of no instance in which the well-established Greek pattern of low output and high prices, low investment and high profits has been challenged."[7] The Greek government also drew criticism from around the world for its high number of executions, mass arrests, extra-judicial killings, and other harsh judicial measures.[8] While these methods did harm to the Greek communists, they also aided Soviet propaganda and repeatedly embarrassed the Truman administration. Right-wing parties dominated the government and labeled all liberals as communists. This dominance of the government by the right, colored many ideas intended to win the support of moderates or non-communist liberals as appeasing communism. After a political crisis in January 1949, a more broad-based government formed that reduced, but did not eliminate the right-wing harassment of liberals.[9]

The Greek Communists

At the beginning of 1948, the KKE and its Democratic Army clearly had the momentum in the war. Despite having suffered significant casualties, recruiting and conscription had increased the size of Democratic Army. It had the initiative and could strike almost anywhere in Greece. Nevertheless, the nationalists decisively defeated the communists in August 1949. The

KKE's continued dedication to fighting conventionally and its rift with Yugoslavia both contributed significantly to this defeat. However, neither of these strategic issues is sufficient to explain the Democratic Army's 1949 demise. Without a nationalist army that could exploit these problems, the communists could have at least maintained control over significant portions of northern Greece.

Markos is Purged-Commitment to Conventional Tactics

The Democratic Army continued its process of conventionalizing its guerrilla army in accordance with Zachariades's strategy throughout 1948. By December 1948, it had established ten light infantry divisions with a supporting bureaucracy.[10] It also continued to expand supporting branches such as artillery, logistical, and engineer units. The field artillery would eventually accumulate nine batteries with approximately sixty howitzers, fifteen 105mm guns and forty-five 75mm guns. They also had over thirty anti-aircraft artillery guns and forty anti-tank guns, in a mix of 20mm and 37mm calibers. Throughout 1948 and into the spring of 1949 the communists sustained this force structure even though the communists' commitment to conventional tactics cost them an enormous level of casualties. Repeated communists assaults on GNA positions in battles like Konitsa, Grammos, and Vitsi cost the communists thousands of casualties. Through volunteers, conscription, and abduction they replaced these losses. By September 1948, they had recovered from their losses in the Grammos campaign and other smaller 1948 battles. The Democratic Army expanded to over 25,000 by 1948 despite an average casualty rate of 2,765 a month, not including wounded.[11] Their organization of approximately 70,000 auxiliaries provided excellent intelligence and makes the guerrilla bands extremely mobile until March 1949, when there was a noticeable decline in support.[12]

Building, organizing, and sustaining this force was an impressive feat for a guerrilla army. However, the rate of attrition from their conventional tactics meant that they were only able to sustain the force structure, not expand it to the 50,000 men that Markos believed was necessary to militarily defeat the GNA. Moreover, the attrition decreased the average quality of the Democratic Army's soldiers and led the KKE to use more violence to enforce conscription. The communists used training areas in Yugoslavia, Albania, and Bulgaria where they conducted basic training and a variety of officer training courses. These training programs could not produce trained soldiers and officers fast enough to keep pace with the attrition. Additionally, the communists did not have any experience with large unit operations. This lack of experience meant that when they attempted operations above battalion level, they suffered from same lack of tactical competence that plagued the GNA. The continual loss of experienced officers made this problem even more acute.

The crux of the problem for the Democratic Army was that it could not match the ability of the nationalist government to generate and sustain a conventional field army. For all of its faults, the nationalist government with US assistance was able to conscript, train, and sustain soldiers in the field more effectively than the nascent communist shadow government. The struggle inside the KKE over tactics eventually resulted in Zachariades purging Markos on 31 January 1949, thereby cementing the Democratic Army's conventional tactics.[13]

While most of the literature focuses on the dramatic major conventional operations, it is important to note that there was an incessant high level of small-scale insurgent activity. For example, according to General Staff reports, in January 1949 elements of the Democratic Army recruited 1,500 fighters, destroyed fifty-four vehicles with mines (including eight trains); laid an additional 867 mines that the security forces discovered; conducted seventy-four demolition operations on bridges, railroads, roads, and other infrastructure; and, conducted 354 intimidation and looting attacks on villages. GNA and NDC casualties during this time were 225 killed, 681 wounded, and 271 missing. After the nationalist victory at Florina and in the Peloponnese in February 1949, these numbers dropped significantly in March: 319 recruits, thirty-four successful mine attacks, 293 mines discovered, 17 demolition operations, and 211 village attacks. The nationalist casualties also dropped to 140 killed, 426 wounded, and 37 missing.[14] This significant drop in insurgent activity and lethality indicates a decrease in the support networks that provided intelligence and logistics. The significant casualties from the communist attacks during the winter 1948-1949 and the increasingly successful government operations also contributed to the decrease in capability. During the first quarter of 1949, the monthly rate of attrition for the communists had risen 4,080 a month.[15] If the government forces had not been able to maintain pressure against the Democratic Army, it could have rebuilt its networks and replaced its losses. The KKE also reduced its ability to sustain its forces by alienating its best ally.

The Macedonian Question-Alienating Tito

The KKE's alienation of Yugoslavia had a deleterious effect on the Democratic Army's ability to sustain combat operations. Yugoslavia had been the most generous supporter of the Greek communists. Marshal Josef

Tito, the President of Yugoslavia, supported the KKE to secure his southern flank after his 1948 split with the Soviet Union. Tito also wanted to reclaim what he saw as Yugoslavian Macedonia from Greece, especially since the people of that area were slavophones who were loyal to the communist cause. Yugoslavian aid had continued but in reduced amounts after its June 1948 expulsion from the international communist movement.[16] This aid even extended to minor combat. On 8 September 1948 a Yugoslavian battalion reportedly fought alongside of a Democratic Army unit in the Kaimaktchelon region near the Yugoslavian border, retaking a mountain that commanded the region's road network.[17]

Yugoslavia's aid diminished greatly during the 1948-1949 winter until it essentially ended by March 1949. There were two principle issues dividing Tito and the KKE. First, Zachariades, as a devout Stalinist, wanted to denounce Tito even though Yugoslavia was helping sustain Zachariades' conventional operations. Second, Zachariades had the KKE's fifth plenum on 30 January 1949 endorse the cause of Macedonian independence. By doing so, he hoped to garner more recruits from the slavophone Greeks. These Greeks had organized their own insurgent organization because the Greek government's policies disadvantaged the slavophone minorities of northern Greece.[18] Moreover, Zachariades believed that Bulgaria would provide more aid in exchange for supporting Macedonian independence. When Zachariades purged Markos, he removed the last influential pro-Tito voice in the KKE.[19]

Yugoslavia ended its aid by March 1949 and took active measures against the Greek communists after 10 July 1949 when Tito announced the closure of the border with Greece. Tito took these actions not only because of his conflict with the KKE, but also because he was able to get economic benefits from the US and the United Kingdom.[20] Yugoslavia had ended its aid and disarmed guerrillas it found inside Yugoslavia, but the terrain on the border was so difficult that no one could precisely define where the border was, much less control it. Moreover, US intelligence indicated that the Yugoslavians made little effort to close the border. The loss of Yugoslavian aid did compound the attritional problem created by the dedication to conventional tactics.[21] The loss of Yugoslavia's support was not necessarily crippling for the Democratic Army. It still maintained safe havens in Albania and Bulgaria. When Yugoslavia began to curtail its aid in October 1948, Albania became the Democratic Army's main supporter.[22] Moreover, the Democratic Army could have survived if it was still facing the nationalist regime it battled in 1947. By 1949, the nationalists' material and operational improvements magnified the communist errors.[23]

The Material Situation

Although the security crisis in late 1947 had convinced the Truman administration that operational and material military aid had to have priority over economic aid, the economic programs continued. The beginning of the Marshall Plan brought additional economic resources. The military material aid continued to improve the arms and equipment of the Greek armed forces. However, without the constant advice and supervision of the US advisors, the Greek military may not have been able to capitalize on the communists' errors. The reduced budgets and US goals for the mission in Greece make it even less likely that material aid alone could have enabled the nationalist forces to defeat the communists.

Economic Aid

The United States' mission in Greece had helped stabilize the economy and reduce inflation by the second quarter of 1948 and provided critical relief for the millions suffering from the war. The passage of the Marshall Plan in 1948 made the economic aid more efficient by enabling the mission to plan on a four year cycle. The intent of the Marshall Plan was to improve the self-confidence and resistance of democratic Europe to communism. In Greece, the war undermined this laudable psychological goal. The lack of security continued to halt reconstruction and the guerrillas continued to destroy property, interrupt trade, and cause civilians to flee their homes.[24]

A reorganization of AMAG in 1948 increased the efficiency of the economic program. On 15 September, Truman appointed Henry Grady as Ambassador to Greece and Chief of AMAG, which improved unity of command.[25] With only one civilian voice in Athens, the Truman administration had a more consistent message for the Greek government. However, Grady and Van Fleet disagreed on the policy in Greece. Van Fleet thought Grady wanted to give into the communists' demands, while Grady resented Van Fleet's influence and thought that the Greek military was becoming too powerful in Greek politics.[26]

Beginning with the 1949 Peloponnesian operation, the AMAG and JUSMPAG integrated the economic reconstruction and development programs with the military plan, so that the Greek people could see that "the democratic way of life has something to offer them."[27] JUSMAPG and AMAG initiated these programs after military operations cleared an area of guerrillas. The US advisors prioritized the programs in three phases: immediate humanitarian aid, six-month reconstruction projects, and long-term projects. The immediate aid focused mostly on food and lumber. The second phase consisted of six-month projects focused on rebuilding roads, improving government efficiency, and encouraging farmers to return to their land. The third phase was open-ended and included projects that would take longer than six months or required a very secure environment.[28] JUSMAPG issued instructions in March 1949 for its field advisors to have the Greek military "participate actively" with the economic programs, especially with refugees and recently secure mountain villages. The Greek commanders were to dedicate every vehicle not being used for tactical operations to the relief program.[29]

Sustaining the Nationalist Army

The US mission in Greece continued its vast military aid program that sustained and armed the nationalist army. There were three major aspects to the program during 1948 and 1949, the Greek force structure, arms, and logistics. In July 1948, the Greek government surprised Van Fleet with a detailed request for additional material and another manpower expansion at a Supreme National Defense Council meeting when the US Secretary of the Army, Kenneth Royall, was visiting. The memorandum requested a long list of items including additional dive bombers, incendiary bombs, tanks, and chemical weapons. Van Fleet provided the US refusal based on either the enormous expense or the inappropriateness of certain items, like incendiary bombs and chemical weapons. He did endorse the proposed expansion in a letter to the Joint Chiefs on 31 July 1948.[30] The State Department opposed Van Fleet's request because its policy was that the Greek army should not exceed a size sustainable by the Greek economy. Additionally they assumed that a reduction would occur immediately after the Grammos operations. Grady and many other US officials concluded that the Greek officials would not take action to end the war as long as they thought the Americans would continue increasing the size of the GNA.[31]

In addition to repeated requests for force structure increases, The GNA usually kept more soldiers in uniform than was authorized through various accounting measures. The JUSMAPG was aware of these counting maneuvers, and repeatedly addressed the issue with the General Staff but to no avail. After a February 1949 General Staff request for 50,000 more troops, the JUSMAPG instead agreed to stop counting certain categories of soldiers, including the politically unreliable category "C" personnel who had been detained on an island prison and missing soldiers. The General Staff attempted to get an extra 10,000 soldiers by inducting too many soldiers in the January 1949 draft, but the JUSMAPG forced the GNA to pay for these extra men.[32] Instead of increasing the GNA's size, JUSMAPG did support another measure to increase the level counterinsurgent manpower. Since the GNA used the NDC in more of an offensive role and less for defending their villages, they requested authority to arm civilian home guards. To maximize the combat power for the 1949 campaigns, Van Fleet authorized the GNA to create a Home Guard organization to assume the NDC's village defense responsibilities. Van Fleet also provided 15,000 rifles on the condition that the GNA closely supervise the entire program.[33]

The expansion of the nationalist forces led to a decline in training quality for the army and the NDC. The NDC rapidly expanded from forty-two to ninety-seven battalions in the five months from January to May 1948. This rapid expansion caused problems, such as when an officer and seventy-two soldiers from one battalion "willingly surrendered" to the enemy.[34] Following a suggestion from JUSMAPG, the General Staff decided to use the remaining 1,500 authorized positions to form headquarters and support units for the NDC instead of three additional battalions. They did this because the JUSMAPG advisors noted that the NDC suffered from a lack of leadership and logistical support.[35] On 24 April 1948, JUSMAPG delivered a reorganization plan for the NDC to ease the leadership difficulties and give the platoons more combat power by consolidating the number of maneuver units from four to three at the company and battalion levels.[36]

A high rate of personnel turnover compounded the problems of expansion. There was an 80 percent turnover in the Roumeli and Peloponnese NDC battalions by June 1948. To improve the NDCs' performance, JUSMAPG convinced the General Staff to replace older NDC soldiers with newly trained young men who could presumably better keep up with the regular soldiers.[37] The JUSMAPG officers called the retention of younger soldiers the revitalization policy. The revitalization of the NDC was complete by June 1949, making those battalions more capable of fighting alongside the GNA. Revitalization extended to the GNA, where the US advisors convinced the General Staff to adopt personnel policies that released older soldiers, kept young ones in service longer, and emphasized the induction of educated middle and upper class men.[38]

The rapid expansion of the army also reduced unit effectiveness. The Greek General Staff shortened basic training so that it could get soldiers into its units faster, especially during the times when the United States authorized a temporary over-strength, such as during the six months from March to September 1948. One of the best demonstrations of the decline in average unit quality was when a company from the communist Youth battalion successfully assaulted a nationalist battalion on 4 March 1948.[39] The JUSMAPG, noting the drop in training time and quality, had its field teams attempt to improve unit training.[40]

JUSMAPG also sought to strengthen nationalist combat power by requisitioning specific weapons that would prove useful in the mountains, aircraft, machine guns, 75mm howitzers, and recoilless rifles. The JUSMAPG put a high priority on air power and procuring aircraft to enable the RHAF to conduct air strikes. In 1948, this meant Spitfires. For the final 1949 campaigns, JUSMAPG acquired Helldivers from the US Navy. As noted above, the Berlin airlift and other priorities took precedence over the RHAF. On 27 April 1949, the US Air Force halted all requisitions for the RHAF.[41]

For the army, there were three weapons that the US advisors thought were critical for improving nationalist combat power. First, the advisors believed that they had to increase the number of light and heavy machine guns in the GNA. In 1947 and early 1948, the communists actually had more machine guns in many battles. To do this, they added a machine gun company to each division. Second, JUSMAPG increased the number of 75mm "pack" howitzers in the GNA. The pack howitzers were easier to maneuver in the mountains and could be carried by the gunners into firing position. Third, after the communists demonstrated that they were capable of building reinforced pillboxes JUSMAPG ordered 75mm recoilless rifles for the 1949 campaigns. Even though these weapons required vehicles for transportation, the advisors believed that their ability to destroy bunkers was critical for the final operations. European Command transferred eight systems to Greece and sent a training team.[42]

In addition to improving nationalist firepower, JUSMAPG put significant effort to improving the GNA's logistics. The US mission supplied the Greek with air-drop parachutes, C-47 cargo planes, and seven all-weather landing strips to improve its Aerial resupply capability. It added 7,500 trucks to the Greek logistical system. The trucks could move supplies into forward depots, which the US advisors supervised, but they usually could not make it to the front lines in the mountains. To solve this problem, JUSMAPG overhauled and expanded the Greek pack animal program. The advisors established an army school for animal handling, managed herds, controlled the selection of soldiers for the program, purchased special radios and saddles, and bought thousands of mules from outside of Greece. JUSMAPG benefited from the fact that the US Army still had soldiers and officers with extensive horse cavalry and mule experience. Despite the US efforts to provide enough war material for the nationalist army, they still had to resort to rationing artillery rounds in 1949. Reduced budgets contributed to the need to ration the nationalists' ammunition consumption.[43]

Reduced Budgets for the US Mission

Throughout 1948 and 1949, the Truman administration continually reduced the budget requests from the advisors in Greece. Budget negotiations in Washington resulted in a reduction of the initial JUSMAPG budget for July 1948 to June 1949 from 250 million dollars to less than 200 million. The Congress reduced the initial authorization by fifty million in the annual Appropriations Act.[44] JUSMAPG's budget request for the next twelve months was initially 450 million, which JUSMAPG argued was necessary to achieve a decisive victory at the earliest possible date. Budget negotiations reduced this sum to 200m.[45] Negotiators from the Departments of State, Army, Navy, and Air Force made this reduction based on what was affordable before there was any input from Greece. The Department of the Army told JUSMAPG to prepare a plan for a further 25 percent cut depending of the position of the Bureau of Budget. Furthermore, the new guidance was that the US aid would be based "on an austerity basis" and available "only to the extent required to eliminate large scale guerrilla activity." The US would not support a Greek effort to control its northern border. If the approved level of aid proved insufficient, the administration would not authorize any increases. Only a potential communist "position of dominance" would justify additional support.[46]

Although the United States was still providing a significant amount of military and economic aid, the US officials in Greece realized that the administration was not willing to provide extra funding to achieve a decisive victory. The long-term goal remained reducing the size of the Greek military to a size that the Greek economy could sustain. This led to the conclusion that the advisors had to emphasize using the available manpower efficiently.[47] The advisors reminded their counterparts of the "urgency of putting every available man in [the] attack for maximum pressure across the entire front."[48]

The Greek National Army and the US Advisors

Despite its increasing material superiority, the nationalist army was unable to fulfill the hopeful expectations for a decisive victory in 1948. The US advisors in JUSMAPG, under a new commander, continued their efforts to instill aggressive leadership, sound tactics, and diligent control during battle. Through extensive training efforts, mentoring Greek officers, close supervision and direction, disciplinary action, and the support of a new Greek commander-in-chief, the advisors were able to improve nationalist battlefield effectiveness. The decisive victories of 1949 demonstrated this new found combat prowess.

Lieutenant General Van Fleet Arrives

Lack of progress in war led the Army to replace Livesay with a more aggressive officer, James A. Van Fleet, who was promoted to Lieutenant General before he arrived in Greece.[49] He commanded the 8th Infantry Regiment, 90th Infantry Division, and III Corps during World War II.[50] Van Fleet brought a definite change in tone to JUSMAPG. While Livesay pushed his advisors to make the Greeks more aggressive, he had also told his advisors "we must remember that we are not in a position to demand."[51] Even after pushing for more authority to provide operational advice, he chose to not give advice on the relationship between the army and the gendarmerie on 4 November 1947.[52] In contrast, Van Fleet later categorized himself as having been a "dictator, a military dictator in every meaning of the word."[53] The Prime Minister and King Paul, who had ascended to the throne after his brother George II died in June 1947, gave Van Fleet their full support. In his own description of how he advised the Greek military he says he always respected Greek sovereignty. Instead of always dictating orders, he used a softer approach. In an interview Van Fleet described his soft approach by describing how he would bring a plan to the that he wanted the GNA to execute. He told the Greek officers, "here is a wonderful plan that has been worked out by your staff with my staff's concurrence. We ask that you approve it and we'll execute it together."[54] By several accounts he was a charismatic leader who easily inspired the Greek soldiers. Moreover, while he could be very critical and demanding of Greek officers, he would also speak very warmly about Greek leadership in public and send florid congratulatory notes to successful commanders.[55]

Van Fleet quickly focused on the lack of aggressive leadership as one of the critical problems in Greece. In dismissing an effort by the US Air Force to establish a helicopter unit to conduct air mobile operations, Van Fleet said that getting to the enemy locations was not the problem, it was getting "them to move out promptly after they get there."[56] In one of his first episodes with the Greek government, he criticized the Minister of War for having a battalion secure his vineyards in the Peloponnese, while allowing the guerrillas to maintain a stronghold in the mountains five miles away.[57] Van Fleet saw to it that his advisors would aggressively fix Greek combat leadership.

The 1948 Campaigns

A series of battles in February and March 1948 did not substantially alter the status quo. It began well for the nationalists with a month long operation to fix and destroy an insurgent unit of approximately 1,200 in the plains around Mount Olympus in central Greece. The operation eventually caught the majority of fighters, although it was a lightly armed unit.[58] Another operation, in the Naousa region in late February succeeded in taking a guerrilla base, but only after the guerrillas had routed two NDC battalions.[59] In the third major operation, two brigades from VIII Division, supported by a commando group, attempted to clear a portion of the Epirus region to prepare for future operations in the spring and summer. After meeting some initial success, driving communist units into Albania, the offensive stalled. A counterattack on 5 March "stampeded one Greek battalion into retreat and caused the entire GNA force to withdraw to their original positions."[60] At the end of the month, on 29 March, two brigades in the Krousia Mountains surrounded a guerrilla unit three times, only for the guerrillas to escape each time. The US advisors noted a failure of commanders to move forward where they could control the battle, not maintaining unit integrity, not maintaining a reserve, and ineffective use of artillery.[61]

The next month, the GNA met with more unqualified success with Operation Dawn, the Roumeli operation that the JUSMAPG advisors drove the General Staff to make happen. From their positions in Roumeli, approximately 2,000 communist regulars were able to interdict all of the roads leading out of the Athens region, isolating the capital from all land transportation. Two GNA divisions attacked on line from the west while a third division attacked from the north, trapping the insurgent formation against the Gulf of Corinth. The JUSMAPG advisors declared the operation a success, with the nationalists claiming 751 guerillas killed and 1,761 captured for a nationalist cost of 42 killed, 68 wounded, and 44 missing. According to the official JUSMAPG history, the operation caused to "entire Greek nation to regain confidence in the ability of their army to defeat the enemy."[62] This operation defeated a major threat to the economic health of Athens and all of Greece.

The JUSMAPG advisors for A Corps and the three divisions conducted a review of the Roumeli operation and concluded that there were several deficiencies. The US advisors concluded that the Greek commanders had difficulty using their staff efficiently, were still using the double-battalion concept, and routinely violated unit integrity. Maneuver units had demonstrated that they could not integrate fire and maneuver, made little effort at concealment or security, and were "reluctant to maintain contact with the enemy especially after dark."[63] Nevertheless, the Roumeli operation revealed modest improvements in aggressive pursuit and battlefield control of maneuvering units.

The JUSMAPG advisors intended to follow the Roumeli success with an operation against the main communist base in the Grammos Mountains, but they were not yet able to get the Greek General Staff to be able to plan one operation while it was executing another. While the advisors and the General Staff prepared the next major operation, several small battles occurred that showed continued problems in the nationalist military. An I Division operation that began on 26 May allowed most of the guerrillas to evade when the commanders hurried their units to stick to a fixed timeline. The quick pace did not allow the soldiers any time to search for hidden guerrilla locations while they swept through the area.[64] In June, a guerrilla unit overran a GNA battalion and the 76th Brigade headquarters that had been securing a road into the Grammos region.[65]

Meanwhile, US advisors assisted in creating the operation order for Grammos, inspecting and making corrections in the logistical preparations, and preparing B Corps for the operation.[66] The plan called for B Corps to seize the Grammos region with six divisions. To encircle the estimated 7,500 communist regulars in the Grammos region, IX Division attacked from the southwest and XV Division would attack from the northeast. The four remaining divisions cleared the encircled area in a generally northern direction. On 16 June 1948, XV and IX Divisions began the battle with their offensives to prevent an enemy retreat into Albania. Stubborn communist resistance blocked XV Division on the 20th and the IXth on 25 June. The Corps commander shifted I Division north to assume XV's mission while the other divisions began their clearing operations. I Division made progress, but a strong line of pillboxes and counterattacks on 10 and 18 July checked the advance. The guerrillas had constructed pillboxes out of logs that were impervious to nationalist bombs and artillery. "Fanatic enemy resistance" stopped two of the other divisions. The faltering progress induced the General Staff to order A Corps to assume command of the southern sector, allowing B Corps to focus on the north.[67] The potential of a stalemate also motivated the US advisors to increase the pressure on the Greek commanders. Van Fleet instructed his advisors to "insist on constant heavy pressure over [the] entire front." The Greek divisions needed "a more aggressive attitude and a rapid advance."[68]

Continued pressure from both the northern and southern sectors, with divisions advancing one ridgeline at a time, eventually resulted in the two corps linking up on 3 August. By 5 August, the two corps secured the ridges along the Albania border, but the communists still defended the Grammos strongholds in force. On 10 August, the nationalist forces resumed the attack, using their British tanks in frontal attacks. A series of divisional attacks gained momentum as the divisions cleared the outer defensive positions around Grammos, resulting in the 20 August capture of a major portion of the Grammos ridge. The remaining insurgent forces retreated the next day, breaking through the nationalist lines into Albania.[69]

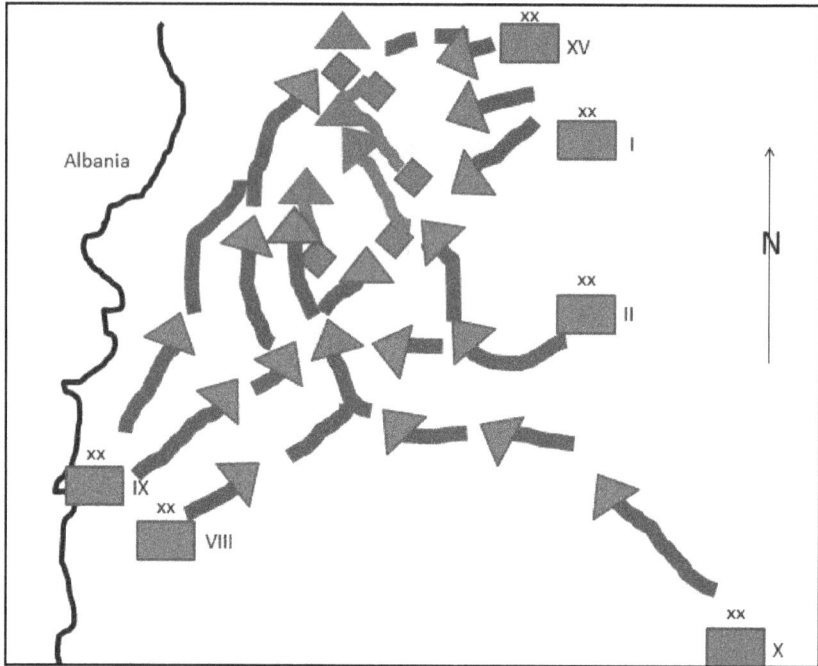

Figure 2. Sketch of the 1948 Grammos Campaign

Source: The author created the map based on the information found in US Army, *JUSMAPG*, map enclosed between pages 84 and 85.

The nationalist forces uncovered vast stores of war material in the Grammos ridge complex, including a hospital, a printing plant, and ministerial offices for the communist shadow government. The GNA claimed to have killed 2,590 enemy fighters, and captured 1,060 (616 of which surrendered). The nationalists suffer 5,824 casualties: 801 killed, 4,961 wounded, and 62 missing. Because the General Staff and JUSMAPG had hoped that the Grammos campaign would decisively end the war, they were disappointed despite having attrited an estimated 16 percent of the Democratic Army.[70] The Greek civilian morale was also low across the country after the Grammos campaign because it failed to achieve the lofty goals publically set for the operation.[71] The official JUSMAPG history acknowledges that the advisors underestimated their enemy.[72]

The US advisors conducted a review of the operation to identify weaknesses in the nationalist army. The critiques can be divided into two categories, the art of command and tactics. The Greek commanders did not have a solid grasp of the art of command, specifically, how to command and control their units on the battlefield. The senior officers and their staffs were inefficient at coordination and staff work. Subordinate commanders "frequently disregarded" orders from their superiors. The US advisors also observed excessive caution in the Greek commanders. The Grammos review specifically cited commanders not advancing without "overwhelming air and artillery support" or spending extra time securing their flanks.[73]

The advisors believed that the weaknesses in tactics centered on a persistent inability to integrate fire and movement, the cornerstone of infantry tactics. The US advisors also felt that Greek reconnaissance and night operations were weak, resulting in Greek commanders declining to patrol or move at night. Conversely, the US advisors characterized the junior officers and soldiers as brave under fire and could endure "long periods of physical hardship."[74] Their courage when attacked notwithstanding, the junior officers could not effectively maneuver on the battlefield.

The General Staff gave B Corps little respite to work on these weaknesses. On 18 August, the General Staff ordered B Corps to occupy the captured Grammos area and seize the Vitsi Mountains, which 4,500 guerrillas had fortified to replace their lost positions in Grammos. The plan called for a five-brigade attack to seize a series of ridges and mountains near the Albanian border on 30 August. After a slow start caused by the rugged terrain, bad weather, and strong resistance, B Corps committed an additional division with three brigades. By 5 September, the southern two brigades had moved within two kilometers of cutting the insurgents' supply route from Albania. This led the insurgents to mount a vigorous counterattack on 10 September that forced the nationalists to retreat back to their 30 August starting positions.[75]

Three days later, the General Staff responded by ordering another division to reinforce B Corps and instructing the B Corps commander to prepare his forces to resume the attack.[76] While the nationalists reinforced and prepared, the communists attacked again on 20 September against II and XV Divisions, forcing salients three kilometers deep into the GNA's lines. This attack disrupted the GNA operations, but cost the communists an estimated 600 casualties. Van Fleet flew to the B Corps headquarters with the senior British officer in Greece and the Greek Chief of the General Staff, General Dimitrios Yiadzis to pressure the corps into aggressive action to break the apparent stalemate. "Working closely with their JUSMAPG counterparts," the corps staff generated a new plan for X Division to seize key terrain from the south, while the other two divisions conducted supporting attacks. After an initial bombardment, the first day's offensive met with minimal resistance. That night, however, communist artillery fire induced one brigade to fall back three kilometers to its starting position. The rest of the units followed suit.[77]

The General Staff took over planning and formulated a new plan.[78] They transferred two commando groups from the Peloponnese and made them the main effort. The B Corps divisions would conduct supporting attacks to encircle insurgent positions before the commandos attacked the dug-in positions on the Vitsi Mountains. Minefields and counterattacks stopped the divisions' "listless efforts," but the commandos were able to seize the heights.[79] Continued fighting produced no major results except additional casualties until a 4 November communist attack seized a key ridge from the 35th Brigade. The brigade momentarily retook the ridge before retreating after nightfall. The General Staff committed the commandos to retaking the ridge, which they did, but at a high cost. The Vitsi operations had cost the commandos fifty percent casualties. This was the last major operation of the Vitsi campaign as an early snow on 20 November 1948 covered the mountains and brought a halt to all major operations, although there were still daily small-scale engagements.[80]

The GNA reported losing 329 men killed, 1,714 wounded, and 145 missing. It estimated that it had killed 1,184 guerrillas and captured 517.[81] The US advisors saw the operation as a failure, in part because they understood the need to end the war as soon as possible.[82] The US Army intelligence assessment in October 1948 was pessimistic because the GNA had been unable to destroy the Democratic Army in the Grammos and Vitsi operations. This inability heightened the tension between the economic requirement to reduce the size of the Greek military and the military requirement to defeat the communists.[83] These conflicting priorities led JUSMAPG to intensify its focus on improving the combat efficiency of the Greek military.

JUSMAPG's review was very critical of the Greek performance. The senior advisor with B Corps, Colonel J. F. Brittingham, wrote that while the plan was sound, "elements were launched piecemeal and at no time were more than three battalions of the corps actually in contact with the enemy."[84] The commanders were "unwilling to attack against even light resistance."[85] The US advisors increasingly criticized the Greek soldiers' morale and will to fight. The root of this problem was the "unwillingness or inability of leaders to command their troops."[86] The US defense attaché concluded after the Vitsi campaign that since increasing manpower would not ensure that the Greek commanders would use that extra manpower efficiently, "the suppression of such activity can be accomplished more economically by correcting demonstrated deficiencies such as, in leadership, combat efficiency and morale."[87] The budget reductions clearly communicated to the US military forces in Greece, that the Truman administration saw "economy in guerilla suppression [was] more important than speed."[88] If the Greek commanders knew how to build cohesive and competent combat units, then the morale problems would lessen. If the commanders knew how to manage their units in battle, then the tactical problems would lessen. The disappointment of the Vitsi campaign swiftly led to a JUSMAPG push to correct the problems so that the GNA would be ready for a spring offensive after the snows had cleared. The JUSMAPG plan focused on training, aggressiveness, tactics, and how to command units in battle.[89]

Training the Nationalist Army

Recognizing the need to improve unit training in the nationalist army, JUSMAPG created a new section in July 1948, the Organization, Training, and Equipment Section. This section oversaw several initiatives to improve Greek combat effectiveness. First, in cooperation with the remaining British officers, the section lengthened basic training from six to seventeen weeks, allowing eight weeks for specialty training after a common basic training for all soldiers. Third, they also monitored a quota system for all units, ensuring that the commanders filled every available slot for junior officer and noncommissioned officer training. Fourth, the section coordinated a program for sending officers to the United States and the United Kingdom to attend formal military schools. After the Vitsi campaign, the section undertook a special program to rebuild the XV Division, which suffered greatly during the Grammos and Vitsi fighting.[90]

While the basic training program was important, JUSMAPG's main training effort was the demonstration platoons. JUSMAPG established ten demonstration platoons, each drawn from a different division. Each platoon was a Greek infantry platoon and a mortar section with a Greek commander, a US army officer, and a British military advisor.[91] The platoons spent a month in specialized training run by JUSMAPG officers that focused on infantry tactics. On 1 October 1948, the platoons returned to the divisions and began a training program there. Every battalion in the division had to complete a sixteen-day field exercise with the demonstration platoon, working up from section to battalion level operations under US supervision.[92]

The advisors encountered numerous Greek officers who were reluctant to conduct training. Some believed that their soldiers did not need training after they had been in combat.[93] Other commanders, such as the commanders in X Division, were not energetic enough in ensuring all of their soldiers were getting the maximum amount of training. In January 1949, Brigadier General Reuben Jenkins, the Assistant Director of JUSMAPG, ordered his advisors to review what every soldier in X Division was doing to determine his availability for training after one of the brigade commanders said his unit was too busy to conduct training.[94] This order was a part of a larger JUSMAPG initiative to maximize training before the 1949 campaigns to improve on the mediocre 1948 campaigns. A 5 January 1949 instruction told all field advisors to submit names of Greek officers who were not fully cooperating with the training programs.[95] JUSMAPG gave special attention to B Corps since it had the most difficulties during the 1948 campaigns. Jenkins' instructions to the B Corps commander included requirements for the corps commander to issues orders to every commander to platoon level to conduct training and the staff to establish a training inspection program. His message for the corps commander also stated that Jenkins intended "to get this army better trained if I have to take the names of recalcitrant officers to the Minister of War to get action."[96]

Influencing the Greek Officers

The JUSMAPG advisors sought to make the Greek officer corps more aggressive, give it a better grasp of tactics, and enable it to control units on the battlefield more effectively. The advisors used three methods to achieve these goals: daily mentorship, direct orders, and disciplinary action. By October 1948, the nationalist army was still not displaying a desire to close with the enemy. "The army has little offensive spirit . . . [and] has proven itself unwilling to the type of aggressive warfare needed to end the struggle." One cause is a failure to provide effective leadership at all levels of the military. The second reason, in Grady's assessment, was that the nationalist army was waiting for the United States to win the war, instead of taking that responsibility upon itself.[97] "Greek leaders have shown in the past few months an increased hesitation to take determined action with forces available as long as there appears to be a possibility that at some future date larger forces may be available."[98]

The JUSMAPG advisors at the division and corps echelons repeatedly pushed their Greek counterparts on conducting more "night movements and night attacks, in emphasizing active patrolling to discover vulnerable spots in the enemy defenses, and in urging Greek units to quickly exploit an enemy withdrawal."[99] The advisors continued one of the central parts of the US program, increasing the aggressiveness of the nationalist forces. The senior JUSMAPG officers frequently sent messages to the field detachments to get their counterparts to attack, "seize [the] advantage with powerful blows on entire front."[100] JUSMAPG believed that it had to push generals who were not the main effort to conduct any operations at all. The guidance to these reluctant Greek commanders was to "seize the opportunity now repeat now" to "cover [their units] with glory."[101] One US report observed that the Greek soldiers always seemed to fight harder when foreign observers were present.[102] The tenacious JUSMAPG insistence on aggressiveness bore fruit in January 1949 when a US advisor observed that the General Staff was "increasingly insistent on continuous pursuit of guerrillas by GNA commands regardless of [unit] boundaries."[103] Another example of success was a General Staff inquiry into why A Corps had delayed a pursuit, thereby allowing a guerrilla unit to escape.[104]

In a short message to all of the US field detachments, Jenkins provided a useful summary of what the US advisors saw as the "basic essentials" of tactics:

All divisions must be highly alert especially at night. Reconnaissance must be constant. Hold maximum possible reserves mobile, ready for rapid movement. Tactical integrity of reserves is vital. Commands must be prepared to ignore tactical boundaries and take offensive on moment's notice either on own account or to support a neighbor. Several alternate plans must be ready for instant implementation and must be known by all important subordinates.[105]

The JUSMAPG advisors constantly drove their Greek counterparts to conduct more aggressive patrolling and intelligence collection. One example is the battle of Karditsa on 11 December 1948, where approximately 1,500 guerrillas overran a GNA battalion and a NDC battalion to plunder the prosperous town. Jenkins used the incident to prod the General Staff into an investigation and overhaul of the GNA's reconnaissance and security procedures.[106] A month later, another communist attack seized the city of Naousa on 12 January 1949. Despite intelligence indicators that an attack was coming, the garrison, which included a brigade headquarters, conducted no reconnaissance or security operations. The C Corps headquarters failed to respond in an organized manner, committing units without any attempt to coordinate their movements. Units that did arrive at Naousa, failed to attack the communists aggressively. As a result, the communists destroyed three-quarters of the town and plundered all the supplies they could carry. JUSMAPG again pushed to punish those responsible for the negligence that enabled the communists to surprise the nationalist garrison.[107] The US advisors were also more assertive in giving orders in the aftermath of these defeats. On 19 January 1949, Van Fleet issued orders to B Corps to pursue two guerrilla divisions. He specified the lines of operation for XV Division and the 71st Brigade and stated that "there will be no excuse for weather obstacles since such do not exist for the bandits."[108]

The field detachments developed solid relationships with their Greek counterparts. The advisors lived with their counterparts in the field, sharing danger and hardship. As a result of the shared experience, they developed a "friendly partnership" which they could use to mentor the Greek officers. During the Grammos operation, the US officers believed that "in most cases Greek commanders asked their advice and acted on their recommendations." The advisors "supervised the planning of all operations," ensuring that the plan adequately integrated fire support and that "aggressive pursuit plans were included."[109] The US advisors also took the lead in planning all operations because every Greek-planned operation was compromised by security leaks.[110] One of the advisors would then accompany the Greek commander during the mission to provide advice and observe the operation. This advisor would write the after-action review, which became "the basis for remedial action by the GNA commanders."[111]

The US advisory efforts paid off the next month on 11 February 1949, when a communist division attacked the II Division at Florina. II Division, following a new defensive plan proposed by the JUSMAPG advisors that included a strong reserve, fought off the communist attack for two days. The commander committed the reserve to reinforce positions against the communist attacks. While the GNA did not pursue the withdrawing communists as vigorously as a US advisor urged, they had killed over 600 and captured 350 enemy fighters at a cost of 55 dead and 252 wounded. The defense of Florina was an example of how the persistent mentorship and training by the advisors could deliver battlefield results.[112]

Improving Greek control of their units in battle was a long process of mentoring commanders and staff officers. It also included forcing staff officers to coordinate with other units and writing plans that made control easier. Staff officers saw coordination as a waste of time and inter-service rivalry inhibited cooperation between the services. Van Fleet corrected this through "advice and personal conference" and "corrective action" by the General Staff advisors.[113] The advisors worked to get the corps and division staffs to accomplish basic tasks that would improve their ability to control units in battle. For example, the advisors at the corps level worked to get the staffs to track the course of battles, maintaining constant awareness of where all their subordinate units were located. The advisors also faced a constant struggle to get Greek units routinely to maintain a tactical reserve and unit integrity whenever possible.[114] The US advisors found that they had to monitor Greek logistical units and staffs constantly to ensure that the Greek officers were exercising due diligence. This constant effort would prove successful when the nationalists were able to push supplies to units to sustain the offensive during the final 1949 campaigns.[115] They also used this same type of tight supervision and direction to ensure that the different Greek military services cooperated. This effort eventually paid off when the RHAF proved more responsive during the 1949 campaigns, conducting aerial resupply, casualty evacuation, and close air support.[116]

When mentorship, or direct instructions, from an advisors failed, the US officers also tried to influence the Greek officer corps by having unaggressive or incompetent commanders disciplined or relieved and then controlling who the replacement process. Van Fleet came to the conclusion that the ineffective leadership of the B Corps commander, Lieutenant General Kalageropoulos, was part of the cause of the slow progress during the Grammos operation.[117] At a 27 July meeting of the Supreme National Defense Council, Van Fleet recommended that the government relieve Kalageropoulos.[118] At a special meeting the next day the Prime Minister asked Van Fleet to nominate a successor. Van Fleet's response was the corps' Deputy Chief of Staff for Operations, Lieutenant General Kitrilakis, which initiated several days of political objections. The Greek cabinet acquiesced when Kalageropoulos submitted his resignation and appointed Kitrilakis as his replacement. The incident shows the incredible level of influence JUSMAPG had acquired in the Greek government and one of the most effective methods it had for improving the quality of Greek military leadership. Van Fleet intervened to effect Kitrilakis's relief less than a month later when "it became obvious that his vacillation would cost precious lives and time."[119]

In another incident, Van Fleet had the General Staff relieve a general when, at the last minute, the general changed the US plan for an attack by ordering a four hour barrage. Van Fleet would later recall scolding the general on the spot for delaying the attack even though the enemy was not firing on the nationalist troops. According to Van Fleet this was the French World War I influence on the Greek army.[120] The General Staff replaced the II Division commander during the Vitsi operation after a two battalion attack routed one of his brigades and two other brigades fell back under communist pressure on 24 October 1948.[121] In a third example, the 74th Brigade commander was relieved during the 1949 Peloponnesian campaign for ordering an unauthorized withdrawal from a hill his brigade had seized.[122] The efforts of the US officers to improve Greek combat leadership did not have instant success, but they were able to improve gradually the overall combat performance of the nationalist army. The advisors' task became easier early in 1949 when new leadership in the Greek military fully embraced the US program.

Field Marshal Papagos Takes Command

On 21 January, King Paul with cabinet confirmation after promoted General Papagos to Field Marshal and appointed him as the Commander-in-chief of the Greek armed forces. The order also abolished the Supreme National Defense Council, reducing political oversight and micromanagement of the military.[123] King Paul made Papagos his personal military advisor until he garnered the political support to put him in command. Papagos enjoyed a popular reputation based on his victory against the Italians and his years in a German prisoner camp during World War II. Papagos immediately issued orders "calling for the manifestation of an offensive spirit that would wipe out the bandit plague."[124] He also recalled two generals, one to be an Inspector General to enforce discipline and the other to be the new Chief of the General Staff.

Van Fleet reported that he had a very strong working relationship with Papagos, who asked Van Fleet for his advice on how to proceed to defeat the communists.[125] Van Fleet responded with a list of proposals that summarized what JUSMAPG was already doing, urging that Papagos support them and enforce compliance by Greek officers. The JUSMAPG director asked Papagos to ensure that the Greek commanders accepted and implemented the unit training plans, the training schools accepted US supervision, and officers in the field operated more aggressively. The first test of the relationship between Papagos and his US advisors came when the C Corps commander refused to allow an investigation into his command's poor performance during a communist winter attack at Naousa. The General Staff ordered the investigation at the behest of the JUSMAPG advisors. Papagos ordered the investigation to continue and threatened the corps commander with court-martial. With the authority of the newly created commander-in-chief position, Papagos overcame the interference of politicians in military affairs. Previously, influential politicians could have been able to protect their favored generals. Papagos' power and his acceptance of his advisors' advice meant that JUSMAPG would have a greater ability to affect Greek leadership throughout the entire military.[126]

Van Fleet reported seeing an increased level of energy in the General Staff by 28 January 1949 in response to Papagos' instructions.[127] On 15 February, Papagos issued orders to eliminate idleness, faintheartedness, and negligence. He declared that every commander "had the authority to shoot on the spot anyone under his command who showed negligence or faintheartedness." Brigade and division commanders could relieve and court-martial officers for failing in their duty.[128] Under his watch, the General Staff published a new manual entitled "Suppression of Irregular (Bandit) Operations" that codified the ideas of aggressive leadership and infantry tactics that the JUSMAPG advisors had been pushing since 1947.[129] The emphasis on aggressive action brought results in 1949 as the nationalist forces finally destroyed the remaining major communist units.

The 1949 Campaigns

The Greek armed forces began 1949 with a new campaign on 3 January to destroy all of the guerrilla units in the Peloponnese, which had been a major security problem since August 1947. The General Staff believed that the communists' 3rd Division had 2,600 regulars and 2,500 armed auxiliaries throughout the peninsula. A Corps and its JUSMAPG advisors had been planning the operation since 29 November 1948. The General Staff assigned fifteen NDC battalions, all of the local gendarmerie, and four commando groups to A Corps for the operation. Additionally the Royal Hellenic Navy assisted with naval gunfire and a blockade of all shipping. The plan included two major differences from previous campaigns. First, gendarmerie arrested every suspected communist sympathizer, estimated at 5,000, as a preliminary step before the GNA began its clearing operations to deny the enemy intelligence and support.[130] Second, the local police, gendarmerie, and NDC would follow immediately behind the methodical GNA clearing operations, reestablishing police stations and local security to prevent guerrillas from returning.[131]

The operation began well after the gendarmerie detained over 4,297 suspected communists and interred them on an island.[132] Four GNA divisions progressed south, focusing on careful clearing instead of rapid movement. The JUSMAPG insistence on maintaining a reserve and planning for pursuit operations paid off on 16 January when a communist battalion attempted to break through the GNA line and evade toward the north. Elements from the 41st Brigade were standing by as the reserve. They pursued the communists and destroyed the unit. While the majority of the force cleared the area from north to south, the commando groups were attempting to pursue and fix the major guerrilla units in the southern part of the peninsula. These efforts met with little success except one operation by two commando groups at the village of Ayios Vassilios. The commandos conducted a night movement over a snow-covered mountain range, which enabled them to surround the village and attack at dawn, destroying a reinforced communist battalion. The progress continued as the GNA moved south. By 25 March only an estimated 250 guerrillas had escaped death or capture.[133]

The balance of casualties heavily favored the nationalists, who lost 56 killed, 173 wounded, and two missing. The General Staff reported killing 1,640 and capturing 2,712 regulars. Additionally, in a sign of increasing momentum for the government, 1,568 communist auxiliaries surrendered during the operation.[134] The JUSMAPG advisors noted that performance had improved, but that Greek commanders still showed insufficient aggressiveness. Nevertheless, the nationalists had achieved a clear-cut success, which greatly benefited from the US operational advice and training.

While the nationalists had success in the south, the Democratic Army launched a large-scale raid on the town of Karpenision in central Greece on 18 January 1949. The communist 2nd division captured the town on 21 January. Three nationalist brigades fought to retake the town, but they failed until 9 February, by which time the communists had destroyed almost the entire town and abducted 1,300 civilians. The nationalists pursued the communists, but frustrated their US advisors by refusing to move faster on account of the snow and counterattacks. The pursuit continued until 28 February when the nationalists could no longer maintain contact with the enemy. Van Fleet and Jenkins both told Papagos and the General staff that the GNA commanders on the ground were responsible for the ineffective nationalist operation. Jenkins' memorandum plainly stated that the guerrillas were able to strike wherever they chose against a better fed and equipped nationalist army because the Greek officer corps lacked a "sense of responsibility, duty, and aggressiveness to win battles."[135]

Despite the poor showing at Karpenision, the nationalists seized the initiative through their success in the Peloponnese and the defense of Florina as discussed above. The GNA spent March and April consolidating their gains and pursing small guerrilla elements. On 1 May 1949, following Van Fleet's vision for a series of operations from south to north, A Corps initiated Operation Rocket with the intent to clear central Greece. B Corps supported the operation by containing guerrilla forces in the northwest, while C Corps conducted small scale operations to maintain pressure on the insurgents in the northeast. The operation showed an improved ability for the higher echelons to manage the battle by breaking into multiple phases, each of which successively isolated and cleared a portion of central Greece while blocking forces interdicted fleeing guerrillas. The US advisors were pleased with the level of aggressive pursuit by their Greek counterparts, which kept the guerrillas on the move, unable to rest or resupply.[136] Whereas the JUSMAPG message traffic from August 1948 to February 1949 showed increasing urgency and desire to impart aggressiveness into the Greek officers, by June 1949 their messages congratulated the Greek commanders on the success of their aggressive operations.[137] The US officers still pushed their counterparts "to keep up the heat" on the communists, but there was a definite shift in tone that indicates increasing satisfaction with Greek battlefield performance.[138] The General Staff reported that nationalist operations from April to June 1949 had inflicted over 10,000 casualties, reducing the estimated communist strength to approximately 17,000 fighters, the lowest level since October 1947.[139]

The General Staff and JUSMAPG had begun planning for the next operation, named Torch, while Rocket was underway. The plan for Torch envisioned an offensive by four divisions and five commando groups to clear first the Vitsi area and then the Grammos Mountains. Since the first Vitsi campaign the General Staff had been using the commando groups more and integrating them more effectively with the regular divisions.[140] The US officers tightly controlled the logistical preparations for the final operation. They spent weeks supervising the stockpiling of depots in forward locations so that supplies could be pushed forward to the front line units, instead of those units having to drive to distant warehouses.[141] On 10 August 1949, the operation commenced with two pincer attacks to encircle the estimated five communist brigades and a frontal attack by two divisions and two commando groups. As a result of the weakening Democratic Army and the improved nationalist combat leadership, the assaults broke through the communist lines in three days. While the nationalists showed better combat leadership, the US advisors still provided operational mentoring and direction throughout this operation. They continued to cajole the Greek commanders into aggressive action and worked to synchronize the plans of various units.[142] The survivors of the communist units hastily withdrew toward Albania with the GNA in pursuit. The General Staff estimated that it had destroyed two brigades and attrited the other three by 50 percent.[143]

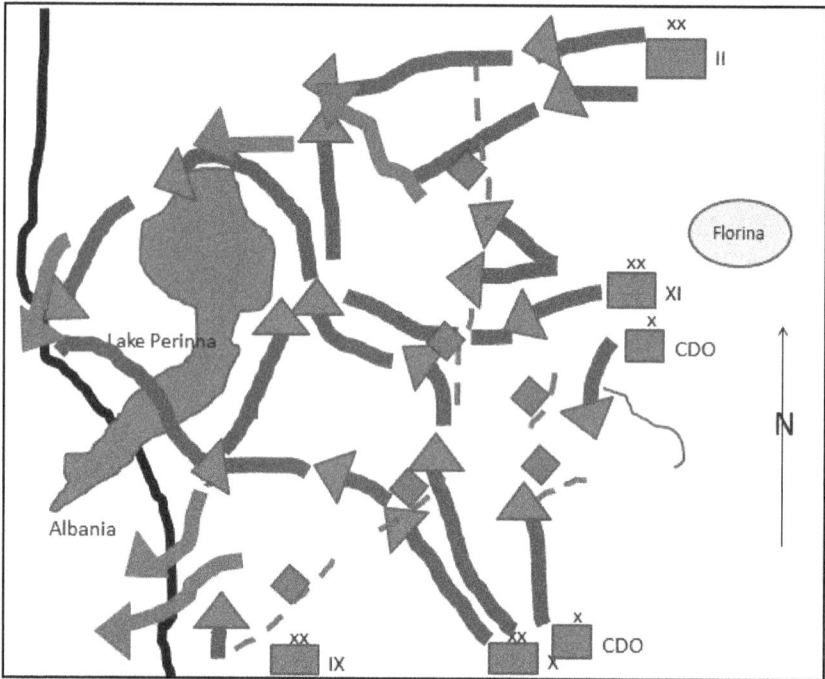

Figure 3. Sketch of the 1949 Grammos Operation

Source: The author created the map based on the information in US Army, *JUSMAPG: Brief History*, map enclosed between pages 19 and 20.

Leaving two divisions to consolidate the victory and prevent a communist return, the commandos and two divisions turned south toward Grammos to begin the second phase of the operation on 24 August. Two fresh divisions also contributed to the operation. IX Division enveloped the Grammos positions from north to south down the border with Albania while VIII Division maintained blocking positions in the south. The remaining forces assaulted the communist positions on the ridge lines. Using the US advisors' training in night operations, the attack began under cover of darkness. As in the Vitsi phase of the operation, the improved aggressiveness, tactics, and command of the nationalist forces enabled the GNA to break through the communist defense in three days. Once the remaining units of the Democratic Army collapsed and began their disorganized retreat, the nationalists pursued for two days until they reached the Albania border. Van Fleet reported a decisive victory in his situation report on 29 August 1949.[144] They spent a month tracking small groups of guerrillas, searching the mountains, and salvaging as much material as possible until 21 September when the General Staff declared an end to the operations. While several hundred scattered communist fighters remained in Greece, Operation Rocket was the decisive end to the threat from the Democratic Army. The GNA arrayed several divisions along the border to defend against external aggression and sent two divisions to a new JUSMAPG training program to prepare them for new missions. JUSMAPG eventually retrained all of the Greek armed forces to prepare them for their role in the defense of Western Europe by the North Atlantic Treaty Organization.[145]

Summary

The JUSMAPG advisors improved the combat leadership of the nationalist army through persistent training, mentorship, direction, and disciplinary action. With more aggressive commanders, better tactics, sound battlefield control, and adequate logistics, the GNA maintained constant pressure on the Democratic Army. Under constant threat from the nationalists, the communists could not recover from their battlefield losses or their own errors. The advisor's influence over the operations and leadership of the Greek Army proved critical to the decisive nationalist victory.

Notes

1. Dean Acheson, "Conversation with the President" 19 April 1949, Dean G. Acheson Papers, Box 65, Memorandum of Conversation Files, Truman Library 3374; Department of State, Memorandum of Conversation, "Overriding Priority for $125,000,000 China Aid," 16 November 1948, General Records of the Department of State, National Archives and Records Administration, College Park, MD, Records Group 59, Records of the Officer-in-Charge of Greek Affairs, Subject File 1946-1951, Box 39.

2. War Department, Cable 7744 to USAGG, Athens, 16 April 1948, Records of Interservice Organizations, Joint United States Military Advisory Group Greece, Records Group 334, Entry 146, Incoming and Outgoing Messages, Box 92; James Van Fleet, Cable to Chief of Staff, USAF, 17 December 1948, Records of Interservice Organizations, Joint United States Military Advisory Group Greece, Records Group 334, Entry 146, Incoming and Outgoing Messages, Box 114; US Air Force, Cable to USAGG, Athens and USAFE, 26 May 1948, Records of Interservice Organizations, Joint United States Military Advisory Group Greece, Records Group 334, Entry 146, Incoming and Outgoing Messages, Box 92.

3. James Van Fleet, "Interview with General James A. Van Fleet," Interview 3, Tape 3, 56.

4. George Marshall, Memorandum for Mr. Lovett re Athens Visit, 20 October 1948, General Records of the Department of State, National Archives and Records Administration, College Park, MD, Records Group 59, Records of the Officer-in-Charge of Greek Affairs, Subject File 1946-1951, Box 39; National Security Council, "NSC 5/4, The Position of the United States with Respect to the Use of US Military Power in Greece," 3 June 1948, Records of the Army Staff, Plans and Operations Division, National Archives and Records Administration, College Park, MD, Records Group 319, Entry 154, Decimal File 091, Box 14; Jones, 133-134, 206-213.

5. Jones, 141.

6. Gallager, 258.

7. John O Coppock, "Greece–End of 1948," John O. Coppock Papers, Harry S. Truman Presidential Library, Box 1, 2.

8. Department of State, "Greek Executions and Internal Security Measures," General Records of the Department of State, National Archives and Records Administration, College Park, MD, Records Group 59, Records of the Officer-in-Charge of Greek Affairs, Subject File 1946-1951, Box 39.

9. Department of State; Jones, 162; Averoff-Tossizza, 313-317; US Army, *JUSMAPG*, 118.

10. The communists built division level organizations, but could not maneuver a division in the field as a division. Just as the nationalists experienced

difficulties managing large units in battle, the communists did not have the depth of experienced staff officers and commanders to fight a division. The leap from raids and ambushes to division-level combined arms maneuver is very difficult.

11. Shrader, 111-114.

12. Department of State, Minutes of the Meeting of the Executive Committee, 14 January 1949, James A. Van Fleet Papers, Military History Institute, Carlisle Barracks, PA, 1. 6483; US Army, *JUSMAPG*, 107; Shrader, 93-96; US Army, *JUSMAPG: Brief History 1 January 1948-31 December 1949*, Records of Interservice Organizations, Joint United States Military Advisory Group Greece, Records Group 334, Entry 154, Historical File, Box 146, 24.

13. Kousouslas, 252-253, 260-261; Averoff-Tossizza, 317-322; Shrader, 110-114, 263-265.

14. United States Army Group-Greece, "Quarterly Report For Period Ending 31 March 1949," General Records of the Department of State, National Archives and Records Administration, College Park, MD, Records Group 59, Records of the Office of Greek, Turkish, and Iranian Affairs, Subject File Greece-Turkey 1947-1950, Box 21.

15. US Army, *JUSMAPG: Brief History*, 24.

16. Intelligence Division, "The Greek Guerrillas' System of Supply," *Intelligence Review*, no. 96 (18 December 1947): 18-19, Archives: Military History Institute, Carlisle Barracks, PA.

17. US Army, *JUSMAPG*, 110.

18. Kousoulas, 263-264.

19. Shrader, 182-186; Kousoulas, 263-264.

20. Shrader, 184-186; Dean Acheson, "Memorandum of Conversation with Sava Kosanovic," 1 July 1949, Dean G. Acheson Papers, Box 65, Memorandum of Conversation Files, Truman Library; "Export License for Yugoslav Blooming Mill," 21 July 1949, Dean G. Acheson Papers, Box 65, Memorandum of Conversation Files, President Harry S. Truman Library.

21. The loss of Yugoslavian support may have created a sense of urgency that reinforced the KKE's decision to win the war conventionally. They needed to win rapidly before the loss of Yugoslavian aid forced them to curtail operations.

22. Shrader, 193-194.

23. Department of State, "Comment on Draft S/P Position Paper RE US Combat Troops in Greece," 29 October 1948, General Records of the Department of State, National Archives and Records Administration, College Park, MD, Records Group 59, Records of the Officer-in-Charge of Greek Affairs, Subject File 1946-1951, Box 39; Van Fleet, "Interview with General James A. Van Fleet," Interview 3, Tape 3, 43.

24. Gaddis, 36-37; Jones, 172; American Mission for Aid to Greece, Monthly Report of the Chief of AMAG to the Secretary of State, 15 April 1948, General Records of the Department of State, National Archives and Records Administration, College Park, MD, Records Group 59, Records of the Office of Greek, Turkish, and Iranian Affairs, Subject File, Greece-Turkey 1947-1950, Box 21, 12; State Department, Meeting of the Executive Committee, 3 September 1948, James A. Van Fleet Papers, Military History Institute, Carlisle Barracks, PA, 2.

25. US Army, *JUSMAGG: History 25 March 1949-30June 1950*, Records of Interservice Organizations, Joint United States Military Advisory Group Greece, Records Group 334, Entry 154, Historical File, Box 146, 1.

26. Van Fleet, "Interview with General James A. Van Fleet," Interview 3, Tape 3, 37-41.

27. Department of State, Meeting of the Executive Committee, 25 February 1949, James A. Van Fleet Papers, Military History Institute, Carlisle Barracks, PA, 2.

28. Department of State.

29. Reuben Jenkins, Cable to Chief JUSMAPG HMC Peloponnese, Love 2948, Records of Interservice Organizations, Joint United States Military Advisory Group Greece, Records Group 334, Entry 146, Incoming and Outgoing Messages, Box 115.

30. James Van Fleet, Cable to Director Plans and Operations, 23 July 1948, Records of Interservice Organizations, Joint United States Military Advisory Group Greece, Records Group 334, Entry 146, Incoming and Outgoing Messages, Box 114; US Army, *JUSMAPG*, 93. The Greek government had asked for poison gas. The documents do not specify if the Greeks asked for specific chemical agents. Van Fleet responded that military chemical weapons were unconscionable and riot control agents like tear gas were ineffective in war.

31. War Department, Cable 87907 to USAGG, Athens, 21 August 1948, Records of Interservice Organizations, Joint United States Military Advisory Group Greece, Records Group 334, Entry 146, Incoming and Outgoing Messages, Box 93.

32. US Army, *JUSMAPG*, 123, 126-127.

33. Department of State, Executive Committee, 14 January 1949, 2-3; US Army, *JUSMAPG*, 134.

34. James Van Fleet, Cable to JUSMAPG Detachment HMG, 16 June 1948, Records of Interservice Organizations, Joint United States Military Advisory Group Greece, Records Group 334, Entry 146, Incoming and Outgoing Messages, Box 113.

35. US Army, *JUSMAPG*, 52.

36. US Army, 80-81.

37. US Army, 81, 83.

38. State Department, Meeting of the Executive Committee, 20 August 1948, James A. Van Fleet Papers, Military History Institute, Carlisle Barracks, PA, 1; Department of State, Minutes of the Meeting of the Executive Committee, 14 January 1949, James A. Van Fleet Papers, Military History Institute, Carlisle Barracks, PA, 2; US Army, *JUSMAPG*, 121, 128.

39. Shrader, 225.

40. US Army, *JUSMAPG*, 51-52.

41. War Department, Cable 97957 to USAGG, Athens, 20 March 1948, Records of Interservice Organizations, Joint United States Military Advisory Group Greece, Records Group 334, Entry 146, Incoming and Outgoing Messages, Box 92; US Air Force, Cable to US Air Force Group-Greece, 26 April 1949, Records of Interservice Organizations, Joint United States Military Advisory Group Greece, Records Group 334, Entry 146, Incoming and Outgoing Messages, Box 94. The use of Spitfires and Helldivers over other aircraft that are more suitable for close-air support or were newer indicates the low priority the British and US governments placed on the RHAF.

42. Stephen Chamberlin, "The Greek Situation: Report to the Chief of Staff," 20 October 1947, Records of the Army Staff, Plans and Operations Division, National Archives and Records Administration, College Park, MD, Records Group 319, Entry 154, Decimal File 091, Box 14, 11; US Army, *JUSMAPG*, 69; Plans and Operations Division, Cable to CINCEUR, 28 June 1949, Records of Interservice Organizations, Joint United States Military Advisory Group Greece, Records Group 334, Entry 146, Incoming and Outgoing Messages, Box 94.

43. War Department, Cable 73119 to USAGG, Athens, 19 April 1948, Records of Interservice Organizations, Joint United States Military Advisory Group Greece, Records Group 334, Entry 146, Incoming and Outgoing Messages, Box 92; US Army, *JUSMAPG*, 69, 93, 131.

44. US Army, *USAGG Vol II*, 25, 34.

45. Ray Maddocks, Cable From Plans and Operations Division to USAGG, 24 November 1948, Records of the Army Staff, Plans and Operations Division, National Archives and Records Administration, College Park, MD, Records Group 319, Entry 154, Decimal File 091, Box 15.

46. Plans and Operations Division, Cable 80149 to USAGG, 26 November 1948, Records of Interservice Organizations, Joint United States Military Advisory Group Greece, Records Group 334, Entry 146, Incoming and Outgoing Messages, Box 93.

47. Department of State, Meeting of the Executive Committee, 13 August 1948, James Van Fleet Papers, Military History Institute, Carlisle Barracks, PA, 1.

48. James Van Fleet, Cable to Chief B Corps JUSMAPG, 13 July 1948, Records of Interservice Organizations, Joint United States Military Advisory Group Greece, Records Group 334, Entry 146, Incoming and Outgoing Messages, Box 114.

49. Plans and Operations Division, "General Livesay's Replacement by General Van Fleet as Director JUSMAPG and Chief USAGG," Records of the Army Staff, Plans and Operations Division, National Archives and Records Administration, College Park, MD, Records Group 319, Entry 154, Decimal File 319.1, Box 51.

50. Benjamin Taylor, Memorandum for the Department of State, 10 February 1948, Records of the Army Staff, Plans and Operations Division, National Archives and Records Administration, College Park, MD, Records Group 319, Entry 153, Decimal File 091, Box 75.

51. William Livesay, untitled speech, 16 January 1948, William Livesay Papers, Military History Institute, Carlisle Barracks, PA, 4.

52. William Livesay, Diary, 4 November 1947, William Livesay Papers, Military History Institute, Carlisle Barracks, PA, 4.

53. Van Fleet, "Interview with General James Van Fleet," Interview 3, Tape 3, 26.

54. Van Fleet, "Interview with General James Van Fleet," Interview 3, Tape 3, 26.

55. C. P. Rodocanachi, "A Day in the Country with General Van Fleet," James A. Van Fleet Papers, Military History Institute, Carlisle Barracks, PA; James Van Fleet, Message for LTG Tsakalotos, 29 August 1949, Records of Interservice Organizations, Joint United States Military Advisory Group Greece, Records Group 334, Entry 146, Incoming and Outgoing Messages, Box 116.

56. Van Fleet, "Interview with General James Van Fleet," Interview 3, Tape 3, 44.

57. Van Fleet, 9.

58. James Van Fleet, Cable to Director Plans and Operations, Records of Interservice Organizations, Joint United States Military Advisory Group Greece, Records Group 334, Entry 146, Incoming and Outgoing Messages, Box 113; US Army, *JUSMAPG*, 71-72.

59. US Army, *JUSMAPG*, 72.

60. US Army, 73.

61. US Army, 74.

62. US Army, *JUSMAPG*, 75-77.

63. US Army.

64. James Van Fleet, Cable to Joint Chiefs of Staff, 12 June 1948, Records

of Interservice Organizations, Joint United States Military Advisory Group Greece, Records Group 334, Entry 146, Incoming and Outgoing Messages, Box 113.

65. US Army, *JUSMAPG*, 79-80.

66. US Army, 81, 84-85.

67. Reuben Jenkins, Cable to JUSMAPG Detachment B Corps, Records of Interservice Organizations, Joint United States Military Advisory Group Greece, National Archives and Records Administration, College Park, MD, Records Group 334, Entry 146, Incoming and Outgoing Messages, Box 113; James Van Fleet, Cable to Joint Chiefs of Staff, 26 June 1948 and 29 June 1948, Records of Interservice Organizations, Joint United States Military Advisory Group Greece, Records Group 334, Entry 146, Incoming and Outgoing Messages, Box 113; US Army, *JUSMAPG*, 85-88.

68. James Van Fleet, Cable to Chief JUSMAPG B Corps, 12 July 1948, Director Plans and Operations, Records of Interservice Organizations, Joint United States Military Advisory Group Greece, National Archives and Records Administration, College Park, MD, Records Group 334, Entry 146, Incoming and Outgoing Messages, Box 114.

69. US Army, *JUSMAPG*, 86-88; James Van Fleet, Cable to Director Plans and Operations, 21 August 1948, Records of Interservice Organizations, Joint United States Military Advisory Group Greece, National Archives and Records Administration, College Park, MD, Records Group 334, Entry 146, Incoming and Outgoing Messages, Box 114.

70. US Army, *JUSMAPG*, 88.

71. American Mission for Aid to Greece, "AMAG 2588," 21 December 1948, Harry S. Truman Papers, President's Secretary's File, President Harry S. Truman Library, Independence MO, Box 112, 2.

72. US Army, *JUSMAPG*, 88.

73. US Army, *JUSMAPG*, 89-90.

74. US Army.

75. James Van Fleet, Cable to Director Plans and Operations, 20 September 1948, Records of Interservice Organizations, Joint United States Military Advisory Group Greece, National Archives and Records Administration, College Park, MD, Records Group 334, Entry 146, Incoming and Outgoing Messages, Box 114; US Army, *JUSMAPG*, 100-102.

76. James Van Fleet, Cable to Director Plans and Operations, 19 July 1948, Love 1430, Records of Interservice Organizations, Joint United States Military Advisory Group Greece, Records Group 334, Entry 146, Incoming and Outgoing Messages, Box 114.

77. US Army, *JUSMAPG*, 103-104.

78. James Van Fleet, Cable to CSGPO, Love 2006, Records of Interservice Organizations, Joint United States Military Advisory Group Greece, Records Group 334, Entry 146, Incoming and Outgoing Messages, Box 114.

79. US Army, *JUSMAPG*, 105.

80. James Van Fleet, Cable to CSGPO, 20 November 1948, Records of Interservice Organizations, Joint United States Military Advisory Group Greece, Records Group 334, Entry 146, Incoming and Outgoing Messages, Box 114; US Army, *JUSMAPG*, 105-106.

81. These are the only casualty figures available. JUSMAPG used the numbers that the GNA reported and there was no other organization reported casualty figures. There may be error or bias for the casualty figures throughout the war. However, the US advisors would have been able to ensure that there were not excessive errors in the number of captured insurgents, since these prisoners would have been included in future logistical head counts.

82. US Army, *JUSMAPG*, 106.

83. Intelligence Division, "Armed Band Activity in Greece," *Intelligence Review,* no. 50 (14 October 1948): 50-55, Archives: Military History Institute, Carlisle Barracks, PA; Van Fleet, Cable to Plans and Operations Division, 20 September 1948.

84. US Army, *JUSMAPG*, 106.

85. James Van Fleet, Cable to Director Plans and Operations, 22 October 1948, Records of Interservice Organizations, Joint United States Military Advisory Group Greece, Records Group 334, Entry 146, Incoming and Outgoing Messages, Box 114, 6.

86. US Army, *JUSMAPG*, 104.

87. Harvey Smith, Memorandum for the Ambassador, "Guerrilla Suppression," 6 December 1948, General Records of the Department of State, Records of the Office of Greek, Turkish, and Iranian Affairs, Subject File 1947-1950, Box 14.

88. Smith.

89. US Army, *JUSMAPG*, 113.

90. US Army, 113-114.

91. The American officers were captains or majors who had commanded in combat: James Van Fleet, Cable to Director Plans and Operations, Love 1485, Records of Interservice Organizations, Joint United States Military Advisory Group Greece, Records Group 334, Entry 146, Incoming and Outgoing Messages, Box 114.

92. US Army, *JUSMAPG*, 114.

93. US Army.

94. Reuben Jenkins, Cable to Chief JUSMAPG Dets X Division and B Corps, 6 January 1949, Records of Interservice Organizations, Joint United States Military Advisory Group Greece, Records Group 334, Entry 146, Incoming and Outgoing Messages, Box 115.

95. Reuben Jenkins, Cable to Chief JUSMAPG Training Center Kolaki, 5 January 1949, Records of Interservice Organizations, Joint United States Military Advisory Group Greece, National Archives and Records Administration, College Park, MD, Records Group 334, Entry 146, Incoming and Outgoing Messages, Box 115.

96. Reuben Jenkins, Cable to Chief JUSMAPG B Corps, 4 January 1949, Records of Interservice Organizations, Joint United States Military Advisory Group Greece, Records Group 334, Entry 146, Incoming and Outgoing Messages, Box 115.

97. Henry Grady, "AMAG 1613," 22 October 1948, Harry S. Truman Papers, President's Secretary's File, President Harry S. Truman Library, Independence, MO, Box 165, 1-3.

98. Henry Grady, Telegram for the Secretary of State, 4 January 1949, General Records of the Department of State, Records of the Officer-in-Charge of Greek Affairs, Subject File 1944-1951, Box 39.

99. US Army, *JUSMAPG*, 89.

100. Reuben Jenkins, Cable to Chief JUSMAPG Detachment B Corps, 16 July 1948, Records of Interservice Organizations, Joint United States Military Advisory Group Greece, Records Group 334, Entry 146, Incoming and Outgoing Messages, Box 114.

101. Reuben Jenkins, Cable to Chief JUSMAPG HMC Peloponnese, 16 July 1948, Records of Interservice Organizations, Joint United States Military Advisory Group Greece, Records Group 334, Entry 146, Incoming and Outgoing Messages, Box 114; Reuben Jenkins, Cable to Chief JUSMAPG Detachment C Corps, 15 July 1948, Records of Interservice Organizations, Joint United States Military Advisory Group Greece, Records Group 334, Entry 146, Incoming and Outgoing Messages, Box 114.

102. Department of State, Memorandum of Conversation, "Greek Situation," General Records of the Department of State, Records of the Officer-in-Charge of Greek Affairs, Subject File 1944-1951, Box 39.

103. James Van Fleet, Cable to CSGPO, 22 January 1949, Records of Interservice Organizations, Joint United States Military Advisory Group Greece, Records Group 334, Entry 146, Incoming and Outgoing Messages, Box 115, 6.

104. Reuben Jenkins, Cable to Chief JUSMAPG Detachment A Corps, 2 April 1949, Records of Interservice Organizations, Joint United States Military Advisory Group Greece, Records Group 334, Entry 146, Incoming and Outgoing Messages, Box 115.

105.Reuben Jenkins, Cable to Chief JUSMAPG B Corps, 25 February 1949, Records of Interservice Organizations, Joint United States Military Advisory Group Greece, Records Group 334, Entry 146, Incoming and Outgoing Messages, Box 115.

106.US Army, *JUSMAPG*, 143-145.

107.Department of State, Meeting of the Executive Committee, 21 January 1949, James A. Van Fleet Papers, Military History Institute, Carlisle Barracks, PA, 2; US Army, *JUSMAPG*, 160-162.

108.James Van Fleet, Cable to Chief JUSMAPG Detachment B Corps, 19 January 1949, Records of Interservice Organizations, Joint United States Military Advisory Group Greece, Records Group 334, Entry 146, Incoming and Outgoing Messages, Box 115.

109.US Army, *JUSMAPG*, 89, 112.

110.Van Fleet, "Interview with General James Van Fleet," Interview 3, Tape 3, 16.

111.US Army, *JUSMAPG*, 112.

112.James Van Fleet, Cable to CSGPO, 15 February 1949, Records of Interservice Organizations, Joint United States Military Advisory Group Greece, Records Group 334, Entry 146, Incoming and Outgoing Messages, Box 115, 4109; US Army, *JUSMAPG*, 150-153.

113.US Army, *JUSMAPG*, 65.

114.US Army, 153-154.

115.Van Fleet, "Interview with General James Van Fleet," Interview 3, Tape 3, 48.

116.US Army, *JUSMAPG: Brief History 1 January 1948-31 December 1949*, Records of Interservice Organizations, Joint United States Military Advisory Group Greece, Records Group 334, Entry 154, Historical File, Box 146, 20-21.

117.James Van Fleet, Cable to Director Plans and Operations, 23 July 1948, Records of Interservice Organizations, Joint United States Military Advisory Group Greece, Records Group 334, Entry 146, Incoming and Outgoing Messages, Box 114.

118.US Army, *JUSMAPG*, 94-95, 103.

119.US Army.

120.Van Fleet, "Interview with General James A. Van Fleet," Interview 3, Tape 3, 14-15. Whether or not French World War I doctrine influenced the GNA, Van Fleet believed that it had left a lasting impression on GNA tactics.

121.James Van Fleet, Cable to Plans and Operations Division, 30 October 1948, Records of Interservice Organizations, Joint United States Military

Advisory Group Greece, Records Group 334, Entry 146, Incoming and Outgoing Messages, Box 114.

122. James Van Fleet, Cable to CSGPO, 30 April 1949, Records of Interservice Organizations, Joint United States Military Advisory Group Greece, Records Group 334, Entry 146, Incoming and Outgoing Messages, Box 115.

123. US Army, *JUSMAPG*, 119; Van Fleet, "Interview with General James Van Fleet," Interview 3, Tape 3, 43.

124. US Army, *JUSMAPG*, 119.

125. Van Fleet, "Interview with General James Van Fleet," Interview 3, Tape 3, 43.

126. US Army, *JUSMAPG*, 121, 123.

127. James Van Fleet, Cable to CSGPO, 28 January 1949, Records of Interservice Organizations, Joint United States Military Advisory Group Greece, Records Group 334, Entry 146, Incoming and Outgoing Messages, Box 115, 3.

128. US Army, *JUSMAPG*, 125.

129. S. Kitrilakes, *Suppression of Irregular (Bandit) Operations*, Records of Interservice Organizations, Joint United States Military Advisory Group Greece, Records Group 334, Entry 146, General Decimal File, 352.11 to 400.312, Box 67, 1-3.

130. James Van Fleet, Cable to CSGPO, 11 February 1949, Records of Interservice Organizations, Joint United States Military Advisory Group Greece, Records Group 334, Entry 146, Incoming and Outgoing Messages, Box 115.

131. US Army, *JUSMAPG*, 135-137.

132. Van Fleet supported this mass arrest against criticism from the American Embassy and the western press: Van Fleet, "Interview with General James A. Van Fleet," Interview 3, Tape 3, 51-52.

133. US Army, *JUSMAPG*, 137-140.

134. US Army, 140-141.

135. US Army, 147-151.

136. Reuben Jenkins, Cable to Chief JUSMAPG Detachment XV Division, 27 June 1949, Records of Interservice Organizations, Joint United States Military Advisory Group Greece, Records Group 334, Entry 146, Incoming and Outgoing Messages, Box 115.

137. For example see Reuben Jenkins, Cable to Chief JUSMAPG Detachment A Corps, 22 June 1949, Records of Interservice Organizations, Joint United States Military Advisory Group Greece, Records Group 334, Entry 146, Incoming and Outgoing Messages, Box 115.

138. Reuben Jenkins, Cable to Chief JUSMAPG Detachment IX Division, 6 August 1949, Records of Interservice Organizations, Joint United States

Military Advisory Group Greece, Records Group 334, Entry 146, Incoming and Outgoing Messages, Box 115.

139. US Army, *JUSMAPG: Brief History 1 January 1948—31 December 1949*, Records of Interservice Organizations, Joint United States Military Advisory Group Greece, Records Group 334, Entry 154, Historical File, Box 146, 17-19, enclosed maps.

140. For example see James Van Fleet, Cable to CSGPO, 3 June 1949, Records of Interservice Organizations, Joint United States Military Advisory Group Greece, Records Group 334, Entry 146, Incoming and Outgoing Messages, Box 115, 3.

141. Van Fleet, "Interview with Van Fleet," Interview 3, Tape 3, 48.

142. Reuben Jenkins, Cable to Chief JUSMAPG Det B Corps, 8 August 1949, Records of Interservice Organizations, Joint United States Military Advisory Group Greece, Records Group 334, Entry 146, Incoming and Outgoing Messages, Box 115.

143. US Army, *JUSMAPG: Brief History,* 19-20.

144. James Van Fleet, Cable to CSGPO, 29 August 1949, Records of Interservice Organizations, Joint United States Military Advisory Group Greece, Records Group 334, Entry 146, Incoming and Outgoing Messages, Box 116.

145. US Army, *JUSMAPG: Brief History*, 20-22, enclosed maps.

Chapter 5
Conclusions

Insist On Energetic Offensive Action Everywhere.

— Brigadier General Reuben Jenkins, Cable To B Corps

The US mission in Greece contributed to the decisive nationalist victory over the communists through its material and operational assistance. Through its operational assistance, JUSMAPG dramatically improved the nationalists' combat efficiency. Despite these successes, there were two negative long-term outcomes for the GNA from the Greek Civil War. First, the Greek Expeditionary Force for the Korean War demonstrated that the GNA had not institutionalized the improvements in combat leadership. Second, the GNA became increasingly active politically and executed a *coup d'etat* in 1967. Nevertheless, JUSMAPG's efforts improved Greek combat leadership sufficiently to achieve victory by August 1949. This improvement, the communist commitment to conventional operations, and the US material support resulted in the massive attrition of communist forces that led to the final decisive battle. The history of the US advisory mission in the Greek Civil War has important implications for future policy makers and advisors to foreign forces.

Long-term Results

While the combined US and Greek effort had defeated the communist threat, the US advisors did not have a total or permanent effect on Greek combat leadership. In 1950, the Greek government decided to send an expeditionary force to support the United Nations command in South Korea that fought to defeat the North Korean invasion. There were still US advisors in Greece assisting the GNA who would attempt to prepare this force for its deployment to Korea. The advisors found numerous leadership problems that threatened the ability of the Greek Expeditionary Force to be a useful fighting formation. The Greek General Staff eventually reduced the size of this force from a reinforced brigade to a reinforced battalion because it could not find the resources to support a larger organization.[1] The General Staff then filled the battalion with conscripts whom the GNA labeled as volunteers. The officers transferred in and out so frequently in the months leading up to the November 1950 deployment that most of the training was for naught. The US advisors also assumed control of all logistical preparations down to the issuing of uniforms because the General Staff refused to release supplies from the warehouses.[2]

In a 17 November 1950 memorandum, the senior US officer who was working with this expeditionary battalion, Lieutenant Colonel Jack Shannon, detailed its deficiencies and recommended a US run training program in Korea once the battalion arrived.[3] He noted that the Greek commander had put no emphasis on training. The advisors organized and executed the squad and platoon level training, which the Greek units completed adequately. However, the Greek commander shortened the training time available for the companies and battalion. The commander's disinterest in training and preparing for combat also affected his unit. In the advisors' evaluation, the training program had "proved beyond a reasonable doubt that the battalion and company commanders were not capable of administrative or tactical command of their units." The Greek officers also completely ignored the advisors' insistence on training the support units and the staffs.[4] The lack of logistical support, personnel issues, and unwillingness to train may indicate that the Greek government did not put a high priority on the Expeditionary Force.

Despite this inauspicious preparatory phase for the Korean War deployment, the Greek Expeditionary Force eventually proved itself. The United Nations command placed the Greek unit under the operational control of US units. Under the supervision and mentorship of the US army while operating with the 15th Infantry Regiment, the Greek Expeditionary Force performed better than the US advisors in Greece who trained it feared. It is clear from the 15th Infantry's regimental history for the year that the regimental commander used the Greeks to support his US battalions. He gave the most important and difficult missions to the US units and used the Greek battalion to relieve exhausted US units. Nevertheless, the Greek battalion performed well under fire when they relieved US units. During the night of 17-18 June 1953, after it relieved US units that had been exhausted by Chinese attacks, the Greek battalion held its position against an attack by a Chinese regiment. A month later, on 17 July, the Greeks demonstrated that they could also conduct offensive operations. Seven Chinese divisions attacked a Republic of Korea division. The US command committed the 15th Infantry to contain the resulting salient. After it had established its defensive positions, the Greek battalion attacked a Chinese company attempting to maneuver around the allied positions. The Greek offensive blocked the Chinese movement after several hours of fighting. Both of these actions reveal a level of combat effectiveness that the GNA never achieved in 1947.[5]

The legacy of the Greek Civil War had other less positive effects. The emphasis by the Truman administration, the ambassador in Athens, AMAG, and JUSMAPG on defeating the communist threat empowered far-right elements of Greek society and the military. Although AMAG's efforts righted the Greek economy and enabled two decades of consistent economic growth after the Civil War, the US efforts also contributed to the undermining Greek democracy and political freedom.[6] The US had increased the effectiveness of the military and other security services, which reinforced their self-image and confidence as the ultimate guardians of Greece.[7] Extreme right-wing organizations continued to flourish, including those that used terror to attack those they perceived as communists. One of these organizations, an association of GNA officers founded during World War II, exerted an ideological influence over the army that justified an increasing political role for the military. These officers believed that the military was the last protector of Greece. Griswold recognized the danger to Greek liberal government from the military's role in politics after the war. In a 26 July 1948 letter to Secretary of State George C. Marshall, he recommended that Marshall replace Van Fleet after the communists had been defeated. He argued that Van Fleet had the "proper offensive combat psychology" to win the war, but lacked the finesse and subtlety to transition the army to a smaller and less political role.[8]

The US officials in Greece continued to reconcile two conflicting perspectives about Greece. From the security perspective, the Truman administration believed that strong stable government were the most effective bulwark against communism.[9] The urgency of the escalating Cold War reinforced this perspective and gave it precedence over the idea that reforming Greek political and economic affairs would improve the country's resilience against communist subversion. The preference for stability led US officials to condone harsh control measures including mass arrests and martial law.[10] The successive governments of Greece would become more right wing and based on a narrower segment of the population. At times, the United States would advise against this trend, while at other times it would support the rightward drift.[11] In 1952, the US ambassador intervened to change the electoral system to ensure a victory by Papagos, who had created his own party after retiring from the army. Right-wing parties continued to control Greece, even using the military to corrupt elections. The military's political role continued to increase until a group of field grade officers engineered a *coup* on 21 April 1967. This putsch brought military rule until 1974 when a combination of widespread protests and demonstrated military incompetence in facing the Turkish military in Cyprus led to a new democratically elected government.[12]

The US policy in Greece, including the military advisory component, had secured the eastern Mediterranean against communist expansion. Its support of repressive governments eventually resulted in such an atmosphere of anti-Americanism that in the 1970s and 1980s the US embassy warned US nationals to stay away from all crowds.[13] Nevertheless, policy makers can learn from JUSMAPG's successes and failures.

Observations

There are numerous observations that policy makers and practitioners can make from studying the Greek Civil War and the US advisory mission in Greece. First, there is a difficult balance between increasing the capacity of the security forces and preserving liberal democracy. The Greek Civil War polarized Greek society, leading each side to label moderates as the enemy.[14] The result was a government based on a very narrow basis of support. Additionally, right wing terrorists like the "X" organization used extrajudicial terror in coordination with some government officials. If the communists refused decisive conventional combat and focused on long-term development of their political infrastructure, the US support for a narrowly based repressive regime may have failed. The United States did not push the Greek government to heal the divisions that had split Greek society since World War I. If the Greek communists had patiently waited, building their strength as the Greek economy failed and the government alienated the people, then the US effort may have required advisors who combined the zeal to instill aggressive combat leadership with the political subtlety to reform the government and undermine the communist movement.

The JUSMAPG advisors pushed for a more comprehensive counterinsurgency program. The 1949 campaigns, especially the operation in the Peloponnese, revealed improved tactics for destroying the insurgent infrastructure that enabled the communists to sustain their combat power. Through the NDC, home guards, and other paramilitary units, the GNA and JUSMAPG attempted to secure villages against communist attack and infiltration. Because of the need for more infantry for conventional operations, both the GNA and JUSMAPG used these village defense troops to support conventional operations, thereby undermining village security. The communists exploited the weakness of village security, but not as much as they could have had they refrained from committing their combat power to conventional operations. The nationalist campaigns were also weak on other parts of what has become accepted counterinsurgency doctrine. For example, the nationalists effectively had no psychological warfare operation. The US advisors began to encourage the nationalists to establish a psychological warfare capability in January 1949. The nationalists responded enthusiastically to JUSMAPG's plans for conducting psychological warfare, but the advisors noted that the "Greek government seem[ed] not to know what information the Greek people need[ed]."[15]

The US advisors frequently played a very controlling role in the nationalist operations, but it was the Greek riflemen who did the fighting and the dying. JUSMAPG lost only one man killed in action, a pilot who was flying as co-pilot in a RHAF fighter. While the situation had become so dire in late 1947 that the Truman administration discretely studied the option of committing US ground forces, the GNA knew that it would have to carry the burden of fighting the war. This gave JUSMAPG a degree of leverage over the GNA since the Greeks could not expect the extremely limited US personnel to fight for them. JUSMAPG also had additional leverage from the very real possibility that the Truman administration might decide to reduce the level of assistance.

Ambassador Grady noted that the Greek general staff would delay taking the offensive if it thought that it could negotiate an increase in US funding by delaying operations and complaining about a paucity of soldiers.[16] The willingness of the Truman administration to reduce its goals in Greece, reduce AMAG and JUSMAPG funding, and focus on other priorities around the world imparted a sense of urgency into the Greek nationalists. The advisors gained leverage to influence their Greek counterparts as the nationalists realized that they needed the United States more than the United States needed them. This was the opposite situation than in Vietnam, where the United States had staked its reputation on the survival of South Vietnam, thereby surrendering some of its leverage over South Vietnam.

The high quality of the officers assigned to JUSMAPG was also critical to the success of the advisory operation. JUSMAPG benefited from the fact that it had a pool of field grade officers with extensive combat experience in World War II. These officers had successfully commanded in combat. Even with this pool of potential advisors, Livesay, Van Fleet, and the Plans and Operations Division of the Army Staff found that only a minority of officers were fit and available to combat advise foreign forces.[17] They chose to delay filling JUSMAPG vacancies rather than send less-qualified advisors.[18] The principal criteria seemed to have been proven combat leadership, aggressiveness, and graduation from the Command and General Staff College. The requirement for aggressiveness extended to staff officers and logisticians, who frequently found that they had to command staffs and support units, if these supporting elements were to support the combat units. By the final campaigns of the war, the US staff and logistical advisors were in de facto command of the GNA sustainment operations.

If the communists had waged a more irregular war, the US advisors may have required more experience and training on counterinsurgency. These additional competencies could include psychological operations, language, guerrilla warfare, and employing paramilitary forces. A more irregular war would have been less decisive and would have required a greater focus on removing the insurgent infrastructure from the villages. The downside of increasing the requirements on advisors is that it would have made it even more difficult to find qualified personnel. A Greek language requirement alone would have disqualified most of the JUSMAPG advisors. Advising a Greek military that was fighting an irregular enemy would have been difficult for the US because it did not yet have the doctrine for or experience in combating insurgencies. Only a handful of US officers fought with indigenous forces during World War II. Moreover, the US Army did not publish its first guerrilla warfare doctrine until 1951.[19] Without doctrinal guide or organization experience, the US Army would have had trouble creating an advisory mission on the scale of JUSMAPG in 1947 that could develop the GNA's counterinsurgency skill.

The presence of US advisors at the general staff level down to the platoons also increased the ability for the advisors to affect the GNA's combat performance. Advisors at higher echelons censured Greek commanders who obstructed the lower echelon advisors. The advisor chain of command was also able to track unit training, enforce standards throughout the GNA, and provide situational awareness up throughout JUSMAPG. Lower-level advisors were able to ensure that platoons and companies were adequately supporting the advisor-developed plans while higher-level advisors could remove bureaucratic obstacles and provide support to the troops on the ground.

Without the authority granted by the senior Greek officers and politicians, JUSMAPG could not have improved the GNA's combat leadership as rapidly as it did. Even with the almost total support from Papagos in 1949, the advisors were not able to effect a total and permanent improvement. Even after two years of working with the GNA, the advisors still drove the Greek officers to be more aggressive during the final 1949 campaigns. The poor initial leadership of the Greek Expeditionary Force to Korea shows how difficult it may be to create a permanent change in leadership by advisors. With a lot of authority and leverage, advisors may be able to instill dramatic improvements in a short-time frame. To make a permanent change, the advisory mission may have to extend over a much longer timeframe.

At the lower levels, JUSMAPG mostly affected combat leadership through its training programs. The demonstration platoons were the major component of this effort. Two factors led JUSMAPG to build an extensive unit training program. First, the Greek basic training courses were not producing soldiers and juniors officers that could operate in the field with any level of competence. Second, the GNA's rapid expansion dramatically reduced the average quality of its units. The expansion may have increased the military's political influence, but it had a negative effect on the ability of the GNA to defeat guerrillas in combat. The GNA also rapidly expanded the NDC, which frequently resulted in NDC units that failed in combat. Counterinsurgents have attempted to expand the security forces rapidly in other conflicts such as in the Malaya Emergency and currently in Afghanistan. The result has generally been that the expansion decreased the average ability to fight.

The JUSMAPG advisors found that to make the training program effective they had to execute the training themselves and diligently ensure compliance by Greek commanders.[20] A US infantry officer trained each of the demonstration platoons and then supervised the training when those platoons returned to their parent divisions to train the other platoons. The division and corps level advisors tracked which units had completed the training. These advisors would also intervene when they found Greek commanders who showed a reluctance to train. While some of the training programs included critical subjects such as technical training on new equipment and pack animal handling, the major focus was on infantry tactics. This included fire and movement, patrolling, fire support, field craft, and night operations. The GNA demonstrated a marked weakness in these skills, which were critical for infantry units to aggressively pursue the guerrillas.

The advisors used a number of ways to influence their Greek counterparts. They built long-term relationships with the Greek officers by working side by side all day for months. This relationship allowed them to make suggestions, discuss, and inform. The relationship also provided the US advisors with very good understanding of the situation. The division level advisors accompanied units down to platoon level in combat, mentoring combat leaders at all levels. US field grade officers frequently advised Greek company grade officers, but not on a constant basis. JUSMAPG assigned its advisors to the division and corps echelons. These advisors accompanied the subordinate Greek units during operations. This structure worked because the GNA divisions usually did not have all of their units operating simultaneously. JUSMAPG would have needed a more robust force structure to maintain a constant presence below the division level. Nevertheless, the advisors' constant presence allowed them to build relationships with their Greek counterparts. This relationship enabled the advisors to develop the ability of Greek staffs to control units in battle, coordinate plans, and overcome units and service rivalries. The advisors' constant message was to be more aggressive, bolder, and faster in closing with and destroying the enemy.

When patient mentorship was not sufficient, the US advisors took a more directive role. Most of the time, they wrote the operational plans and orders for the Greek operations. JUSMAPG tracked the progress of the operation with individual advisors accompanying tactical units to ensure they adhered to the plan. The advisors also exercised direct control over logistics. They found that the Greeks would not use the millions of dollars of US provided material to efficiently prosecute the war unless US advisors closely monitored the supply system.

An important exception to the direct US role was intelligence operations. While JUSMAPG assigned officers to work with the Greek General Staff's intelligence division, the dearth of archival material about the intelligence cycle indicates that JUSMAPG took a minimal role in intelligence operations. The minimal US role in this vital part of counterinsurgency operations was partially a result of demonstrated Greek proficiency. Van Fleet admired the efficiency of the Greek intelligence services, which produced accurate intelligence about communist activities inside Greece and across the border in Albania, Yugoslavia, and Bulgaria.[21] The clandestine nature of intelligence and the connections between Greek intelligence and right-wing terrorist organizations may have deterred the JUSMAPG officers from operating too closely with Greek intelligence.[22] In intelligence operations, the Greek government benefited from men of initiative and skill, traits in which the GNA was short.

In tactical operations, the US advisors found that mentorship and direction were not always sufficient. In some cases, the US advisors took an even harder line, recommending disciplinary action, or relief, for commanders who were not aggressive or repeatedly chose to ignore their advisors. Even when JUSMAPG did not take action, the advisors extraordinary influence undoubtedly affected the willingness of the Greek officers to listen to their advisors. The ability to influence the Greek general staff and politicians on issues of relieving and appointing general officers enabled the advisors to have more success in their training and mentorship programs. In turn, the massive scale of the US aid program and the potential for the United States to reduce that aid provided the leverage that led to the extraordinary influence that JUSMAPG had over the Greek officer corps.

This heavy-handed US approach to advising the GNA was frequently more of a command rather than an advisory relationship. The US advisors could not have had this level of control of the GNA without its extraordinary leverage over the chain of command. This style also may have resulted in dramatic short-term gains, but undermined the long-term development of Greek combat leadership. By planning operations and logistics for them, the advisors reduced the opportunities for the Greek officers to learn from experience. They violated the advice of Colonel T. E. Lawrence to "not do too much with your own hands."[23] The direct US approach achieved immediate results, but inhibited a sustainable improvement in Greek combat leadership.

Causes of the Nationalist Victory

Strategically, the communists and the nationalists in Greece had similar tasks. They had to control a population, extract resources from that population and external sources, convert those resources into a military force, sustain that force, and then efficiently use that military against their opponent's military, infrastructure, and population. The KKE's two egregious errors, the alienation of Yugoslavia and the commitment to conventional tactics, reduced their ability to execute these tasks. Losing Yugoslavian assistance and safe havens meant that the Democratic Army had fewer resources and fewer places into which it could withdraw for sanctuary. The commitment to conventional tactics increased the Democratic Army's rate of attrition by willingly engaging in tactically decisive battles. The conventional tactics put the Democratic Army in a position where the GNA could destroy it with aggressive conventional operations. While the KKE and the Democratic Army showed incredible dedication and discipline in replacing losses, their losses far exceeded their ability to generate combat power in 1949.[24] The rapid collapse in August 1949 suggests that the average quality of the communist forces had declined significantly, as they attempted to replace losses. In 1949, the communists had an estimated peak strength of approximately 24,000 men but lost an estimated 32,000 casualties from January to September.

This 133 per cent loss broke the communist ability to generate combat forces. If the communists had chosen to refrain from openly contesting territory, using guerrilla tactics while building their political control over the population, then they would have had a much lower attrition rate.[25]

Nevertheless, the communists' errors are not sufficient to explain their decisive defeat completely. If in 1949 the Democratic Army faced the GNA of 1947, then the communist safe havens inside Greece would have been safe because the nationalists did not have the tactical ability to clear and hold those areas. Without dramatic improvements in combat leadership, the GNA could not have inflicted the same level of punishment on the insurgents. Moreover, without better tactics the GNA could not destroy the insurgent infrastructure. This infrastructure consisted of the personnel who controlled the population, garnered resources, conscripted fighters, and collected intelligence. The GNA's improved tactics in 1949, beginning with the Peloponnese campaign, denied large portions of Greece to communist influence and taxation. Additionally, without the JUSMAPG efforts, the GNA would not have pursued aggressively, applied sustained pressure on guerrilla units.

The GNA applied this pressure against the communists partially because of the massive level of US-provided material aid. AMAG supervised an extensive program to rebuild the Greek economy and fund its government. This effort stabilized the economy, enabling the Greek government to govern more effectively. Stabilizing the economy also reduced the recruiting pool for the insurgents. The military aid program clothed, fed, and equipped an expanded nationalist military. The US provided planes, suitable artillery, new weapons, radios, trucks, and mules. These supplies enabled the nationalists to conducted extended operations in rural areas. The GNA could sustain units who were pursuing guerrillas. This kept the pressure on the guerrillas, preventing them from resting and resupplying.

Despite the size of the aid program, it too is not sufficient to explain the nationalist victory and communist demise. The GNA only used its new supplies and weapons to pressure the insurgents when JUSMAPG advisors ensured that they aggressively sought out the guerrillas. Without the advisors' constant insistence on more aggressive action, the GNA would have kept the United States provided material in warehouses. While the material aid increased the GNA's combat power, the advisors enabled the GNA to apply this increased power against the insurgents. Moreover, the economic aid had its greatest effect after the GNA had secured the country through its decisive victory.

JUSMAPG's advisors played a critical role in achieving the GNA's decisive victory. The advisors ensured that the GNA allowed the communists no respite through their tireless driving for aggressive action, better tactics, constant pursuit, efficient staff work, and effective logistics. The advisors' ceaseless training, mentorship, direction, and influence led to the aggressive Greek operations that destroyed the communist threat. The critical components of the advisory effort were aggressive combat leaders as advisors, infantry tactics, long-term relationships with Greek officers, leverage over recalcitrant commanders, advisors throughout the Greek chain of command, control over staff and sustainment operations, and the constant pressure to aggressively close with and destroy the enemy.

Implications and Future Research

While every conflict is unique, the case of the Greek Civil War suggests a model for bolstering governments when combat leadership is one of the regime's weaknesses. The United States is currently conducting efforts to improve the combat effectiveness of other militaries in several countries including Afghanistan. If leadership is one of the critical problems, then the recipient government will probably squander any material aid unless advisors ensure that the local government efficiently used the aid to undermine the insurgency. This is not true of all cases. Not all countries require a major advisory effort—material aid may be sufficient. However, if weak combat leadership is causing the local government to lose the war, the United States could apply some lessons from the Greek Civil War.

First, the United States would need to have a high level of leverage to influence the recipient government's leadership. The United States might acquire this leverage from the level of material aid provided and a willingness to settle for lesser goals if the government to be bolstered does not cooperate. Second, the United States would establish an advisory mission but would not take the onus of combat away from the local government. US forces taking on the burden of combating the enemy can create a moral hazard problem where the local government's forces have little incentive to improve their combat effectiveness because the United States is doing the fighting. Third, the United States should place its advisors throughout the chain of command in combat and sustainment positions with the guidance to improve leadership and staff work at all echelons.

Fourth, the mission should select advisors who combine aggressive combat leadership with a subtle understanding of insurgent warfare. Current and future insurgencies are unlikely to place the majority of their combat power in defensive positions where the government can find, fix, and finish them. Consequently, advisors will need to add expertise in securing the population and destroying insurgent infrastructure to the combat expertise that JUSMAPG's advisors had applied. Only a minority of the military's personnel will meet these qualifications. The Greek Civil War is a case where choosing quality over quantity proved successful.

Fifth, the advisors may need to intervene to relieve ineffective commanders, enforce supply discipline, ensure staff coordination, or even take command of units in combat. JUSMAPG's directive style resulted in rapid improvement in Greek combat leadership, but did not institutionalize those changes. The advisors must learn how to balance direct intervention to accomplish the mission with allowing their local counterparts to fight their own war. The leadership failures of the Greek Expeditionary Force for the Korean War shows that a highly directive style may provide immediate results but may not achieve lasting changes in the organization's culture of leadership. On the other hand, a less directive style in the Greek Civil War may not have improved the GNA performance rapidly enough to stave off at least a partial communist victory such as an autonomous region in northern Greece.

Sixth, the advisors must be capable of mentoring leaders and building cohesive combat units that can execute effective tactical operations. This means that they must know how to train units on infantry tactics including night operations, patrolling, operations in rough terrain, and fire support. This also means that the advisors must be able to supervise commanders, their staffs, and the logistical units. The staffs must be able to plan operations, coordinate those operations, and then track their progress. The logisticians must be able to push enough supplies forward so that the combat units can keep constant pressure against guerrilla units. The advisors may have to focus on pack animals and other non-US techniques that the local government can actually sustain.

Since all wars are unique, policy makers must exercise due diligence when building any advisory mission. Additional research can enable policy makers, advisors, and counterinsurgents to achieve the national goals more effectively. Future researchers studying the Greek Civil War can extend the study of certain aspects of nationalist operations including the commando groups, the paramilitary organizations, amphibious operations, and intelligence operations. Research into other cases could study how to strengthen the security services without undermining democratic ideals. How did or could have advisors in other conflicts improve combat leadership and performance? How have advisors in other conflicts balanced immediate tactical results through a directive style with a less directive style that allowed the locals to take the lead? Under what circumstances is this Greek model not applicable? Future research along these lines has the potential to enable better policy decisions and execution when the US attempts to reinforce a government that an insurgency has besieged. The quality of the security forces' leaders will play a critical role in determining the outcome of any insurgency.

Notes

1. Jack Shannon, "Training of the Greek Expeditionary Force," 17 November 1950, Records of Interservice Organizations, Joint United States Military Advisory Group Greece, Records Group 334, Entry 146, General Decimal File, 352.11 to 400.312, Box 67, 1-3.

2. Shannon.

3. Shannon.

4. Shannon.

5. 15th Infantry Regiment, *1953 Yearbook*, http://www.15thinfantry.org/1953yearbook.html (accessed: 5 November 2012), 10-20.

6. Clogg, 148.

7. John Iatrides, "American Attitudes Toward the Political System of Postwar Greece," in Theodore Couloumbis and John Iatrides, eds, *Greek American Relations* (New York: Pella Publishing Company, 1980), 67-68.

8. Dwight P. Griswold, Letter to George C. Marshall, 26 July 1948, Dwight P. Griswold Papers, Harry S. Truman Presidential Library, Independence, MO, Box 1, 1.

9. Iatridas, "American Attitudes," 68.

10. Iatridas, 65-66.

11. John Iatrides, "Reviewing American Policy toward Greece: The Modern Cassandras," in Theodore Couloumbis and John Iatrides, eds, *Greek American Relations* (New York: Pella Publishing Company, 1980), 12-15.

12. Clogg, 147, 155, 162-168.

13. Iatrides, "Reviewing American Policy," 15.

14. Gerolymatos, *Red Acropolis*, 230.

15. Department of State, "Minutes of the Executive Committee Held 14 January 1949," James Van Fleet Papers, Military History Institute, Carlisle Barracks, PA, 4-5.

16. War Department, Cable 87907 to USAGG, Athens, 21 August 1948, Records of Interservice Organizations, Joint United States Military Advisory Group Greece, National Archives and Records Administration, College Park, MD, Records Group 334, Entry 146, Incoming and Outgoing Messages, Box 93.

17. The shortage of combat leaders would also affect the performance of the US Army at the onset of the Korean War. See Roy Flint, "Task Force Smith and the 24th Division: Delay and Withdrawal, 5-19 July 1950," *America's First Battles* (Lawrence: University of Kansas, 1986), 266-299.

18. Albert Wedemeyer, Letter to James Van Fleet, 24 April 1948, Records of the Army Staff, Plans and Operations Division, National Archives and

Records Administration, College Park, MD, Records Group 319, Entry 153, Decimal File 091, Box 77.

19. Andrew Birtle, *US Army Counterinsurgency and Contingency Operations Doctrine 1942-1976* (Washington, DC: Center for Military History, 2007), 132.

20. US Army, *JUSMAPG*, 114; Jenkins, Cable to Chief JUSMAPG Dets X Division and B Corps, 6 January 1949, Records of Interservice Organizations, Joint United States Military Advisory Group Greece, National Archives and Records Administration, College Park, MD, Records Group 334, Entry 146, Box 115.

21. Van Fleet, "Interview with Van Fleet," Interview Three, Tape Three, 21-25.

22. Van Fleet said "there's a lot of dirty work that goes along when you get into this game and there was a lot of it in Greece." Van Fleet, 24.

23. Thomas E. Lawrence, "Twenty-Seven Articles," *Arab Bulletin* (20 August 1917), http://www.telstudies.org/writings/works/articles_essays/1917_twenty-seven_articles.shtml (accessed 27 November 2012).

24. Shrader, 263-266.

25. Shrader, 117.

Bibliography

Primary Sources: Archives

Acheson, Dean G. Papers. Secretary of State Files, 1945-1972. President Harry S. Truman Library, Independence, MO.

Coppock, John O. Papers. US Aid Mission to Greece, 1949. President Harry S. Truman Library, Independence, MO.

Department of State. General Records of the Department of State. National Archives and Records Administration, College Park, MD. Records Group 59.

Donovan, William J. Papers. Military History Institute, Carlisle Barracks, PA.

Griswold, Dwight P. Papers. Chief, American Mission to Aid Greece, 1947-1948. President Harry S. Truman Library, Independence, MO.

Intelligence Division, War Department General Staff. *Intelligence Review*. Military History Institute, Carlisle Barracks, PA.

Livesay, William G. Papers. Military History Institute, Carlisle Barracks, PA.

Porter, Paul A. Papers. American Economic Mission to Greece 1947. President Harry S. Truman Library, Independence, MO.

Records of Interservice Organizations. Joint United States Military Advisory and Planning Group Greece. Records Group 334 National Archives and Records Administration, College Park, MD.

Records of the Army Staff. Plans and Operations Division. National Archives and Records Administration, College Park, MD. Records Group 319.

Truman, Harry S. Papers. Official File, Greece and Turkey. President Harry S. Truman Library, Independence, Missouri, MO.

———. President's Secretary's Files, Foreign Affairs File. President Harry S. Truman Library, Independence, MO.

———. President's Secretary's Files, General File. President Harry S. Truman Library, Independence, MO.

US Army. Army Intelligence Document Files. National Archives and Records Administration, College Park, MD. Records Group 319.

———. *History of the Joint United States Army Group-Greece*. United States Army Unit Dairies, Histories and Reports, Miscellaneous Units,

Records Group 407. President Harry S. Truman Library, Independence, MO.

─────. *History of the Joint United States Military Advisory and Planning Group-Greece*. United States Army Unit Dairies, Histories and Reports, Miscellaneous Units, Records Group 407. President Harry S. Truman Library, Independence, MO.

─────. Records of the Army Staff. National Archives and Records Administration, College Park, MD. Records Group 319.

Van Fleet, James A. Papers. Military History Institute, Carlisle Barracks, PA.

Primary Sources: Non-archival

15th Infantry Regiment. *1953 Yearbook*. http://www.15thinfantry.org/1953yearbook.html (accessed 5 November 2012).

Association for Diplomatic Studies and Training. *Greece: Country Reader*. http://adst.org/oral-history/country-reader-series/ (accessed 5 November 2012).

Clive, Nigel. *A Greek experience, 1943-1948.* Salisbury: Michael Russell (Publishing), 1985.

Department of State. *Foreign Relations of the United States*. University of Wisconsin Digital Collections. http://digital.library.wisc.edu/1711.dl/FRUS (accessed 10 October 2012).

Gallagher, Hubert R. "Administrative Reorganization in the Greek Crisis." *Public Administration Review* 8, no. 4 (Autumn 1948): 250-258.

Henderson, Jim. *22 Battalion*, The Official History of New Zealand in the Second World War 1939-1945. Wellington, New Zealand: Historical Publications Branch, 1958. http://nzetc.victoria.ac.nz/tm/scholarly/tei-WH2-22Ba.html (accessed 15 November 2012).

Kay, Robin. *Italy Volume II: From Casino to Trieste*. The Official History of New Zealand in the Second World War 1939-1945. Wellington, New Zealand: Historical Publications Branch, 1958. http://nzetc.victoria.ac.nz/tm/scholarly/tei-WH2-2Ita.html (accessed 15 November 2012).

Lanz, Hubert. *German Antiguerrilla Operations in the Balkans*. Washington, DC: Department of the Army, 1954.

Papathanasiades, Theodossios. "The Bandits Last Stand in Greece." *Military Review* 30, no. 11 (February 1951): 22-31.

Woodhouse, Christopher M. *The Struggle For Greece, 1941-1949*. London: Hart-Davis, MacGibbon, 1976.

Secondary Sources: Books

Asprey, Robert B. *War in the Shadows*. Garden City: Doubleday and Company, 1975.

Averhoff-Tossizza, Evangelos. *By Fire and Axe: The Communist Party and the Civil War in Greece, 1944-1949*. New Rochelle: Caratzas Brothers, Publishers, 1978.

Beckett, Ian F. W. *The Roots of Counter-Insurgency*. London: Blanford Press, 1988.

Birtle, Andrew J. *US Army Counterinsurgency and Contingency Operations Doctrine 1860-1941*. Washington, DC: Center for Military History, 2004.

———. *US Army Counterinsurgency and Contingency Operations Doctrine 1942-1976*. Washington, DC: Center for Military History, 2007.

Campbell, M., E. Downs, and L. Schuetta. *The Employment of Airpower in the Greek Civil War, 1947-1949*. Maxwell Air Force Base: Air University, 1964.

Couloumbis, Theodore. *The United States, Greece, and Turkey: The Troubled Triangle.* New York: Praeger Publishers, 1983.

Couloumbis, Theodore, and John O. Iatrides, eds. *Greek American Relations*. New York: Pella Publishing Company, 1980.

Davis, Richard G. ed. *The US Army and Irregular Warfare 1775-2007*. Washington, DC: Center of Military History, 2008.

Department of the Army. *The German Campaigns in the Balkans*. Washington, DC: Department of the Army, 1952.

Department of Defense. US Army Europe. *Partisan Warfare: A Treatise Based on Combat Experiences in the Balkans* (1953), by Alexander Ratclliffe.

Dowell, Cassius M. *Military Aid and Civil Power*. Fort Leavenworth: Command and General Staff College, 1925.

Flint, Roy. "Task Force Smith and the 24th Division: Delay and Withdrawal, 5-19 July 1950." In *America's First Battles*. Lawrence: University of Kansas, 1986.

Gaddis, John L. *Strategies of Containment*. Oxford: Oxford University Press, 1982.

Gardner, Hugh H. *Guerrilla and Counterguerrilla Warfare in Greece.* Washington, DC: Office of the Chief of Military History, 1962.

Gerolymatos, Andre. *Red Acropolis, Black Terror.* New York: Basic Books, 2004.

Greene, T. N. ed. *The Guerrilla-and How to Fight Him.* New York: Frederick A. Praeger, 1962.

Heilbrunn, Otto. *Partisan Warfare.* New York: Frederick A. Praeger, 1967.

Hellenikon Phos. *Why Greece is Still Fighting.* Athens: Hellenikon Phos, 1949.

Hermes, Walter. *Survey of the Development of the Role of the US Army Military Advisor.* Washington, DC: Office of the Chief of Military History, 1965.

Herodotus. *The Landmark Herodotus.* Translated by Robert B. Strassler. New York: Pantheon Books, 2007.

Jones, Howard. *"A New Kind of War:" America's Global Strategy and The Truman Doctrine in Greece.* New York: Oxford University Press, 1989.

Kalyvas, Stathis. *The Logic of Violence in Civil Wars.* Cambridge: Cambridge University Press, 2009.

Kousoulas, D. George. *Revolution and Defeat: The Story of the Greek Communist Party.* London: Oxford University Press, 1965.

Laqueur, Walter. *Guerrilla: A Historical and Critical Study.* Boston: Little, Brown and Company, 1976.

McClintock, Michael. *Instruments of Statecraft: US Guerrilla Warfare, Counterinsurgency, and Counterterrorism, 1940-1990.* New York: Pantheon Books, 1992.

McCuen, John. *The Art of Counter-Revolutionary War.* Harrisburg: Stackpole Books, 1966.

McNeill, William Hardy. *The Greek Dilemma.* Philadelphia: J. B. Lippincott Company, 1947.

Miller, James Edward. *The United States and the Making of Modern Greece.* Chapel Hill: University of North Carolina Press, 2009.

Murray, Williamson, and Allan Millett. *A War to Be Won: Fighting the Second World War.* Cambridge, MA: Harvard University Press, 2000.

Oren, Michael B. *Power, Faith, and Fantasy: America in the Middle East 1776 to the Present*. New York: W. W. Norton & Company, 2007.

Packenham, Robert. *Liberal America and the Third World*. Princeton: Princeton University Press, 1973.

Reinhart Carmen M., and Kenneth S. Rogoth. *This Time is Different: Eight Centuries of Financial Folly*. Princeton: Princeton University Press, 2008.

Roubatis, Yiannis. *Tangled Webs: The US in Greece 1947-1967*. New York: Athens Printing Company, 1987.

Sandler, Stanley, ed. *The Korean War: An Encyclopedia*. New York: Garland Publishing, 1995.

Shafer, Michael. *Deadly Paradigms: The Failure of US Counterinsurgency Policy*. Princeton: Princeton University Press, 1988.

Shrader, Charles R. *The Withered Vine: Logistics and the Communist Insurgency in Greece, 1945-1949*. Westport: Praeger, 1999.

Smith, Richard H. *OSS: The Secret History of America's First Central Intelligence Agency*. Guilford, CT: The Lyons Press, 2005.

Stavrianos, L. S. *Greece: American Dilemma and Opportunity*. Chicago: Henry Regnery Company, 1952.

Sutton, Olive. *Murder Inc. In Greece.* Napa, CA: New Century Publishers, 1948. http://www.marxists.org/subject/greek-civil-war/murder-inc/index.htm (accessed 21 October 2012).

Sweet-Escott, Bickham. *Greece: A Political and Economic Survey 1939-1953*. London: Royal Institute of International Affairs, 1954.

Tucker, Spencer. *Encyclopedia of the Korean War: A Political, Social, and Military History Vol 1*. Santa Barbara: Checkmark Books, 2000.

Vlavianos, Haris. *Greece, 1941-49: From Resistance to Civil War*. New York: St. Martin's Press, 1992.

Warren, Harris G. *Special Operations: AAF Aid to European Resistance Movements.* Washington, DC: Army Air Forces, 1947.

Wittner, Lawrence S. *American Intervention in Greece, 1943-1949.* New York: Columbia University Press, 1982.

Zotos, Stephanos. *Greece: The Struggle for Freedom*. New York: Thomas Y. Crowell Company, 1967.

Secondary Sources: Periodicals, Theses, and Dissertations

Abbott, Frank. "The Greek Civil War, 1947-1949: Lessons for the Operational Artist in Foreign Internal Defense." Monograph, School of Advanced Military Studies, 1994.

Alivizatos, Nicos. "The Greek Army in the Late Forties: toward an Institutional Autonomy." *Journal of the Hellenic Diaspora* 5, no. 3 (Fall 1978): 37-45.

Borchard, Edward. "Intervention-The Truman Doctrine and the Marshall Plan." *The American Journal of International Law* 41, no. 4 (October 1947): 885-888.

Gerolymatos, Andre. "The Road to Authoritarianism." *Journal of the Hellenic Diaspora* 35, no. 1 (Spring 2009): 7-25.

———. "The Security Battalions and the Civil War." *Journal of the Hellenic Diaspora* 12, no. 1 (Spring 1985): 17-27.

Haas, Thomas. "The Communist Army of Greece 1944-1949: A Study of Its Failure." Master's Thesis, Command and General Staff College, 1976.

Hinrichs, Ralph. "United States Involvement in Low Intensity Conflict Since World War II: Three Case Studies—Greece, Dominican Republic and Vietnam." Master's Thesis, Command and General Staff College, 1984.

Kalyvas, Stathis. "The Greek Civil War in Retrospect." *Correspondence,* no. 4 (1999): 10-11.

Kennan, George. "The Sources of Soviet Conduct." *Foreign Affairs* 25, no. 4 (July 1947): 566-582.

Lawrence, Thomas E. "Twenty-Seven Articles." *Arab Bulletin* (20 August 1917). http://www.telstudies.org/writings/works/articles_essays/1917_twenty-seven_articles.shtml (accessed 27 November 2012).

Marazantzidis, Nikos, and Giorgos Antoniou. "The Axis Occupation and Civil War: Changing Trends in Greek Historiography, 1941-2002." *Journal of Peace Research* 41, no. 2 (March 2004): 223-231.

Maude, George. "The 1946 British Parliamentary Delegation to Greece: A Lost Opportunity?" *Journal of the Hellenic Diaspora* 11, no. 1 (Spring 1984): 5-25.

Merrill, Dennis. "The Truman Doctrine: Containing Communism and Modernity." *Presidential Studies Quarterly* 36, no. 1 (March 2006): 27-37.

Nachmani, Amikam. "Mirror Images: The Civil Wars in China and Greece." *Journal of the Hellenic Diaspora* 19, no. 1 (1993): 71-112.

Papadimas, John. "An Overview of the Greek Resistance as a Prelude to the Dekemvriana." *Journal of the Hellenic Diaspora* 22, no. 2 (1996): 11-37.

Sepp, Kalev I. "Resettlement, Regroupment, Reconcentration: Deliberate Government-Directed Population Relocation in Support of Counter-insurgency Operations." Master's Thesis, Command and General Staff College, 1992.

Shrader, Stephen. "British Military Mission (BMM) to Greece 1942-44." Monograph, School of Advanced Military Studies, 2009.

Smith, Clyde A. "Greece and Oman: Successful Ango/American Counterinsurgencies Viewed From Current American Doctrine." Master's Thesis, Command and General Staff College, 2009.

Swissler, John. "The Transformations of American Cold War Policy Toward Yugoslavia, 1948-1951." Ph.d diss., University of Hawaii, 1993.

Van Meter, David C. "The Macedonian Question and the Guerrilla War in Northern Greece on the Eve of the Truman Doctrine." *Journal of the Hellenic Diaspora* 21, no. 1 (1995): 71-90.

Veremis, Thanos, and Andre Gerolymatos. "The Military as a Sociopolitical Force in Greece, 1940-1949." *Journal of the Hellenic Diaspora* 17, no. 1 (1991): 103-128.

Vlanton, Elias. "From Grammos to Tet: American Intervention in Greece and Beyond." *Journal of the Hellenic Diaspora* 10, no. 3 (Fall 1983): 71-80.

www.ingramcontent.com/pod-product-compliance
Lightning Source LLC
Chambersburg PA
CBHW081418090426
42738CB00017B/3410